PERGAMON GENERAL PSYCHOLOGY SERIES

Editors: Arnold P. Goldstein, *Syracuse University*
Leonard Krasner, *SUNY, Stony Brook*

EMOTION IN THE HUMAN FACE:

Guidelines for Research
and an
Integration of Findings

PGPS-11

EMOTION IN THE HUMAN FACE:

Guidelines for Research and an Integration of Findings

PAUL EKMAN

The Langley Porter Neuropsychiatric Institute
University of California School of Medicine, San Francisco

WALLACE V. FRIESEN

The Langley Porter Neuropsychiatric Institute, San Francisco

and

PHOEBE ELLSWORTH

Stanford University

PERGAMON PRESS INC.

New York · Toronto · Oxford · Sydney · Braunschweig

PERGAMON PRESS INC., Fairview Park, Elmsford, N.Y. 10523

PERGAMON OF CANADA, LTD., 207 Queen's Quay West,
Toronto 117, Ontario

PERGAMON PRESS LTD., Headington Hill Hall, Oxford

PERGAMON PRESS (AUST.) PTY. LTD., 19 Boundary Street,
Rushcutters Bay, Sydney, N.S.W.

VIEWEG & SOHN GmbH, Burgplatz 1, Braunschweig

Printed in the United States of America

08 016643 1 (H)
08 016644 X (S)

To:

Robert Berryman
Gordon F. Derner
Robert E. Harris
Margaret Tresselt

Contents

Preface

Our aim in this book is to integrate knowledge about the face and emotion, describing what we know, indicating what we need to know, and providing some guidelines for study of this complicated but intriguing phenomenon. We have both students and researchers in mind as the readers—students not only of psychology, but of anthropology, ethology, sociology, and biology. Although some may be engaged with questions other than those raised here, they nevertheless may profit from knowing the answers to many of the psychological questions which have been asked about the face and emotion; and some of the methods of study might well be appropriate to their own interests in the face. The book should also be useful to students who are not primarily interested in the face and emotion, but who can gain through this book a better appreciation of how a field of behavioral science progresses— the problems, the mistakes—and how experiments conducted over five decades fit together. There is excitement, at least for the writers, as answers emerge.

The second intended audience consists of those planning or already conducting research on the face. While research on the face and emotion was quiescent for some years, in the last few years many new investigators have turned to this topic. This book should provide current information, integrating experiments conducted over a long period of time. Some of the conceptual ambiguities that have hindered research and the methodological decisions which must be made in planning research on the face and emotion are discussed. How past investigators handled these matters is presented critically, and a set of standards is offered, which should at least provoke thought and at best provide guidelines for research.

Our hope is that the reader will be better able to profit from the past and avoid asking questions that have actually already been answered, alerted to the methodological pitfalls into which others have fallen and sensitive to some of the new challenging questions which can be asked. Most of the research analyzed in this book has already been published. But important new findings are reported for the first time and integrated with the past results.

Although we stopped gathering material in the Summer of 1970, the information covered in a number of instances is a few years ahead of scientific publication.

PAUL EKMAN
WALLACE V. FRIESEN
PHOEBE ELLSWORTH

Acknowledgments

My own interest in the face and emotion stems from a longer and broader interest in the whole range of nonverbal behavior—body movements, gesture, and posture, as well as facial behavior. In studying nonverbal behavior I have found it crucial to understand how the information provided by the face may differ from that which can be derived from the body. Reluctantly at first, I was led to focus upon the problem of the face and emotion. My reluctance stemmed from my trust of past reviews of that literature which suggested it was a difficult area of research with only meager findings.

I am grateful to Carol Ammons, editor of the journal *Perceptual and Motor Skills*, who was kind enough to put me in touch with Silvan S. Tomkins after noting the overlap in our interests from articles which each of us had submitted to that journal. Tomkins has taught me much about the face. Watching him interpret facial behavior dissipated my resistance, convincing me that this would be a rich and exciting area for study. In the last few years Tomkins has been a consultant on many experiments and a collaborative investigator on one.

As my own research on the face proceeded, I became perplexed as to why there had been so many failures in the past when I and other current investigators were obtaining positive results. This led me to read with care some of the earlier literature. When I discovered that many of the questions I had been asking had already been answered, but that either the original investigator was not aware of the implications of his data, or his findings had been misreported or ignored by reviewers, the idea for this book began.

I am extremely grateful for the generous support I have received from the National Institute of Mental Health, both from the Research Fellowships Branch and the Clinical Research Branch. After finishing my M.A. thesis on body movement in 1955, I received a predoctoral research fellowship to continue studies of nonverbal behavior. Since that time my research on nonverbal behavior was supported by a post-doctoral research fellowship, a Career Scientist Development Award and research grants from the Clinical

xi

Research branch of NIMH. Some of the experiments reported here and part of the time for writing this book were supported by an NIMH grant MH 11976 and a NIMH Career Scientist Development Award 5-KO2-MH06092.

Much of my thinking about the face and emotion, and certainly some of the most fruitful experiments, developed from a cross-cultural study I have been conducting with Wallace Friesen over the past four years. Lee Huff, formerly Director of the Behavioral Sciences Branch of the Advanced Research Projects Agency, is chiefly responsible for our initiating this cross-cultural research. Lee provided the initial encouragement to counter our fears about embarking upon such a difficult research study, and also authorized the grant support. Some of the experiments reported here and part of the time for writing this book were funded by a grant from the Advanced Research Projects Agency, administered by the Air Force Office of Scientific Research AF-AFOSR-1229-67.

Wally Friesen, one of the authors of this book, has been my close collaborative investigator in studies of nonverbal behavior for the last five years. We have worked together so intimately at every stage of research that it would be difficult to distinguish his ideas from mine. During the preparation of this book Wally provided continual contributions to the theoretical and methodological framework, and helpful criticisms of the manuscript. Phoebe Ellsworth, our other author, provided invaluable aid in the search for relevant experiments, furnishing analytical working papers comparing studies, contributions to the organization of the book, and keen judgments of earlier drafts of this book. A National Science Foundation fellowship provided support for Phoebe during the period she worked on this book. Patsy Garlan has provided prodigious editorial help in the writing, and many useful insights into content. Allen Dittman was kind enough to read an earlier draft, and gave me detailed suggestions and criticisms. My thanks also to our typists, Virginia Stark and Harriet Lukes.

I wish to dedicate the book to the four psychologists who, at different points in my career, gave me the encouragement and opportunity without which I would not have been able to develop my research.

PAUL EKMAN

University of California,
San Francisco
Summer, 1970

Introduction

The human face—in repose and in movement, at the moment of death as in life, in silence and in speech, when alone and with others, when seen or sensed from within, in actuality or as represented in art or recorded by the camera—is a commanding, complicated, and at times confusing source of information. The face is *commanding* because of its very visibility and omnipresence. While sounds and speech are intermittent, the face even in repose can be informative. And, except by veils or masks, the face cannot be hidden from view. There is no facial maneuver equivalent to putting one's hands in one's pockets. Further, the face is the location for sensory inputs, life-necessary intake, and communicative output. The face is the site for the sense receptors of taste, smell, sight, and hearing, the intake organs for food, water, and air, and the output location for speech. The face is also commanding because of its role in early development; it is prior to language in the communication between parent and child.

The *complexity* of the face is apparent when we consider its sending capacity, the information it may convey, and its role in social life. Although there are only a few words to describe different facial behaviors (smile, frown, furrow, squint, etc.), man's facial muscles are sufficiently complex to allow more than a thousand different facial appearances; and the action of these muscles is so rapid, that these *could* all be shown in less than a few hours' time. The face is also a complex information source. We can learn different things from looking at a person's face. The face can send messages about such transient and sometimes fleeting events as a feeling or emotion, or the moment-to-moment fluctuations of a conversation. The face can show more enduring moods, perhaps even stable personality characteristics and traits, and such slow progressive changes as age or state of health, and such immutables as sex. The complication is not just the opportunity to glean such a wide variety of information from this single source, but the possibility of drawing inferences which may not be correct.

1

Certainly physiognomic or environmental factors can result in misinformation from the face—for example, the prematurely wrinkled face in a young person. But the face can also misinform by intention or habit. Although smiles may be a reliable index of pleasure or happiness, a person may also smile to mask a feeling he wishes to conceal or to present a feeling when he has no emotion at all. Is the face like an involuntary system or is it subject to voluntary activation and thus vulnerable to purposeful control and disguise? Clearly, it is both.

The very richness of the face, the number of different facial behaviors, the number of different kinds of information we may derive from observing the face, and the uncertainty about whether we are obtaining correct, incorrect, or even purposefully misleading information, can give rise to *confusion*. How can the movements of the face be described when there is no vocabulary to label them, when there are so many different facial appearances, and when they can change so rapidly? Which of these facial appearances are relevant to learning about a person's emotions, which to learning about his personality? Which will tell us whether he is listening or wants to interrupt us and speak himself? And how can we know when the face is purposefully misleading us?

Our purpose is to clarify such confusion about the face by critically evaluating a body of research to provide answers to some of the questions which have been asked. It will be necessary to restrict our focus, considering only one type of information which can be obtained from the face (information about emotion), from only one type of organism (human adults), considering only one type of evidence (empirical research). The vastness of the research literature, the variety of problems encountered in the study of the face, and the difficult conceptual issues which must be considered in order to integrate the multitude of studies, require these restrictions.

We chose to focus upon questions about how the face provides information about *emotion* because these have been the most frequently asked questions, certainly by investigators, and perhaps also in life when people see each other's faces.[1] The face of the human *adult* was selected because some of the methodological problems involved in work with children and nonhuman primates are quite different, and because there has been much less work on these now rapidly developing areas. And, we will only consider evidence which is based on scientific research (largely in psychology), because our aim is to aid further research by providing a discussion of the obstacles which have impeded it and, most importantly, to provide answers, not speculations, about what we now know about the face and emotion.

---

[1] The reader is referred to Vine, I., "Communication by Facial-Visual Signals," for a review of the face excluding emotion.

Of the many intriguing questions that can and have been asked about the human face and emotion, Part Three will discuss the evidence on seven major lines of research. What words can be used to describe the emotional information which we observe in the face? How many different emotions can be seen? Can we discover not only whether someone feels good or bad, but also whether he is interested or happy, whether he is angry, disgusted, sad, or afraid? Are there types of emotional information which are fundamental to understanding the face, such as how pleasant a person feels, how active, how intense? When people are left to their own devices, how do they usually handle the information about emotion they glean from the face? The research on these questions will be discussed in Chapters XIII and XIV.

Is the information about emotion which can be derived from the face always an accurate measure of how a person feels? How often does the face provide *no* basis for accurate judgments of emotion? How often does the face provide incorrect information? Some people may be poker-faced, or may typically mask their true feelings; does the face provide accurate information about emotion for only some people and not for others? And does one require some special tutoring in order to know how to judge emotion accurately from the face? The research on these questions will be surveyed in Chapter XV.

Which of the movements and wrinkles in the face provide accurate information about a particular emotion? Is there one wrinkle which means sadness, and another which means anger? Does one area of the face, such as the eyes, provide more information, or more accurate information, than other parts of the face? Can we link particular facial movements and wrinkles to particular impressions about emotion? The research on these questions will be analyzed in Chapters XVI and XVII.

How does the face compare to other sources of information about emotion? A face is usually seen in context, that is, with words, voice, body, social setting, etc. Can we really read any information from the face alone, or is most of the information about emotion inferred from this context? If we can read information about emotion in the face, and it differs from that contained in the context (i.e., a sad face shown when a person says, "I feel great"), which is correct? Which will most people believe—face or context? Or will they combine both bits of information in forming a judgment? The research on these questions will be discussed in Chapter XVIII.

How does the facial behavior[2] associated with emotion differ across

---

[2] We have avoided the phrase "facial expressions of emotion," since it implies that some inner state is being manifest or shown externally, or that the behavior is intended to transmit information. Instead we have used the more awkward phrase "face and emotion" or "facial behavior."

cultures? Are there any universal associations between a facial behavior and a given emotion, or is the facial behavior distinctive for anger in one culture not relevant for anger in another culture? Do cultures differ in what makes someone angry or sad or happy? Do they differ in whether members of the culture show or conceal any clues to such feelings in their face? Do they differ in the particular facial movements which will occur when someone is angry or afraid or sad? The research on these questions will be examined in Chapter XIX.

More than five decades of empirical research have addressed these questions. Reading this literature from its early beginnings, we have found that the results were not as negative, contradictory, or chaotic as past reviewers have maintained.[3] Our more optimistic picture, that there are answers to many of these questions, is based in part on a reanalysis of key experiments and an emphasis upon studies which have been ignored. In addition, by examining systematically and in detail the research design and results of certain experiments, we have been able both to correct past misinterpretations of results, and to furnish the basis for discrediting some experiments which have managed to survive past criticism.

To make this fundamental reevaluation of the literature required that we develop a conceptual and methodological framework in terms of which to consider each experiment, for much of the confusion both in the experiments themselves and in past reviews has been due to the absence of any such framework. It is no wonder that such confusion has persisted; the conceptual issues are hazy and complex, and the methodological decisions which must be made in designing research on the face and emotion are difficult and intricate.

Part One will discuss some of the conceptual issues which need clarification. The first difficult conceptual problem is deciding what we mean by *emotion*. How does emotion differ from other facets of human experience? For example, is anger an emotion? If so, how does anger relate to hostile or aggressive behavior? How can we tell when an emotion is experienced? We will see in Chapter I that the lack of a clear definition of emotion has caused much difficulty for those trying to study the face and emotion.

Another difficult conceptual problem is specifying just what we mean by the term *accurate*. How do we know whether information provided by the face is accurate? Is there some one criterion to determine what emotion has actually been experienced? Chapter II will delve into this problem and the ways past investigators have dealt with it.

---

[3] Most notably, Landis (1924, 1929) and Sherman (1927a) in their own research reports, and Hunt (1941) in his review of the literature; also Bruner and Tagiuri, 1954; Tagiuri, 1968.

A third conceptual problem is the varied applicability of the term *generality*. If an investigator obtains evidence that observers can distinguish fear from anger, how does he determine the limits of his findings? A number of different kinds of generality must be considered. Are his findings general to settings other than the ones he studied? Are they general to people other than those similar to the ones he studied? Do they have generality in time, in the sense of showing that the face *often* permits this distinction? Do his findings have generality in the sense that most people could make the same distinction? These applications of the term *generality* will be examined in Chapter III.

Another conceptual problem is to determine the extent and effect of people's ability to disguise and *control* their facial behavior. Does control entail both omitting the sign of a felt emotion and simulating the sign of an unfelt emotion? Does such control occur only in some settings, or only with some people? If people can disguise and control their facial behavior, then how does the investigator determine when facial behavior is genuine and when it is simulated? This will be reviewed in Chapter IV.

The final problem—whether to conceive of the face as a single message system which at a given moment in time can show information relevant to only one emotion, or a multimessage system which can simultaneously show the *blend* of two or more emotions—will be discussed in Chapter V.

Part Two will present each of the decisions which an investigator makes if he is to do research on the face and emotion, reviewing what decisions have been made, and recommending particular solutions. The choice between two alternative research approaches and the relationship between the findings of each will be discussed in Chapter VI. The types of circumstances which may elicit facial behavior relevant to emotion will be evaluated in Chapter VII. In the following chapters, a number of questions about sampling will be considered. How many people need to be studied in order to learn about the face and emotion (Chapter VIII)? How much of the facial behavior of each person should be included and how should that be selected from his total facial behavior (Chapter IX)? How many different emotions should be studied to answer questions about accuracy, or cross-cultural similarities, etc. (Chapter X)? If the research utilizes observers who are to record their impressions of emotion, how many words, categories, or scales should they be given (Chapter XI)? The last methodological decision we will address ourselves to is the selection of a recording technique from a number of alternatives (Chapter XII).

Part Three will present, in separate chapters, the research that has been done and the answers which have emerged to seven different questions about the face and emotion. Part Four will describe some research in progress and the implications of the findings from Part Three for theories of emotion. Lastly, we will summarize what we now know about the face and emotion, and pose the questions awaiting further research.

PART ONE

Conceptual Ambiguities

The lack of a broad methodological or conceptual framework for reviewing research on the face and emotion and the pessimistic attitude which has characterized past reviews have had serious consequences. Errors in experimental design have been repeated, recent experiments have been uninformed or misinformed by relevant past work, and interest has at times lagged because of the seemingly discouraging state of the field. These problems are traceable in part to the nebulous nature of the concept of emotion itself (Chapter I). In part they are due to the disjointed history of research characterized by major, disjunctive shifts of interest, which we may consider in three successive time periods. An unjustified pessimism culminated the first period (about 1914–1940), and was followed by a shift of interest to other issues in the second period (about 1940–1960). When in the third period (about 1960 to the present) many of the issues addressed in the first period came again into vogue, the investigations did not sufficiently profit from either the mistakes or the progress made earlier.

During the first period, the face and emotion was a popular topic in the field of psychology. There were many studies, some by investigators well-known today, although not primarily for their work on this topic: e.g., F. Allport, Goodenough, Guilford, Landis, Munn, Woodworth. Despite differences in variables studied and research designs, most experiments addressed one of two issues: Does the face provide accurate information about emotion? Are the facial behaviors related to emotion innate or learned? For a time, there was considerable argument in the literature, but a pessimistic view became dominant. At the least, the results appeared contradictory, and certain advocates—most notably Hunt, Landis, and Sherman—argued that the face was a poor source of information about emotion. There was no accuracy, either as judged by observers or through direct measurement of the face. What little agreement about emotion could be achieved depended more on knowledge of the eliciting circumstance than on observation of the face. And no evidence for innate elements could be found. Commenting in disbelief on this period of research, Hebb wrote (1946, p. 90), "These studies have led to the conclusion that an emotion cannot be accurately identified by another observer."

The second period of research on the face and emotion saw less research by fewer people concerned with different aspects of the phenomenon. The field became largely defined and known by the work and interest of one man, Harold Schlosberg, the only person to publish consistently. A student of Woodworth, Schlosberg continued Woodworth's (1938) interest in the vocabulary of observers' judgments of emotion from the face; but Schlosberg did not pursue Woodworth's finding that judgments made in terms of emotion categories agreed with actors' intended poses. Instead, Schlosberg (1941, 1952, 1954) developed verbal dimensions which he considered to underlie Woodworth's emotion categories; he later proposed a geometric model of how those dimensions interrelate, which he considered relevant not only to facial behavior, but also to developments in the psychophysiology of emotion. While a few others, e.g., Fulcher, Coleman, and Thompson, published articles during this time challenging, at least in part, Landis' and Sherman's earlier negative findings, each published only once and received little attention. Accuracy and the question of innate versus learned components of facial behavior became dormant issues.

In the third period of research on the face and emotion, covering the last decade, there has been a resurgence of interest, sparked in part by clinical investigators looking for behavioral measures applicable to studies of psychotherapy, by the publication of two theories of emotion which emphasized the face (Plutchik's and Tomkins'), and development of the field of Semiotics (*see* Sebeok, Hayes, & Bateson, 1964). Some investigators have continued the line of study initiated by Schlosberg on the dimensions of emotion relevant or useful in observers' judgments of the face. However, many of the current investigations have revived issues which had been dormant since the first period: issues of accuracy, early development and cross-cultural similarities. Rather than avoiding the methodological pitfalls of that first period and building upon some of its promising positive findings, much current work has seemed either uninformed by the early work or conversely directed toward refuting the legacy of pessimism about the face and emotion.

Because of the lack of an orderly progression in development of research issues, concepts, methods, and findings over these three time periods, no framework has emerged within which a survey of findings might have meaning.

We will attempt to supply such a framework. In the next five chapters we will examine some of the conceptual ambiguities and oversimplifications which have hindered research. In Part Two we will then discuss the methodological problems which have impeded research in the area throughout its history.

CHAPTER I

What Do We Mean by "Emotion"?

Most writers have disagreed in their definition of emotion, often describing different phenomena. Izard (1969), in reviewing the literature, wrote, "The area of emotional experience and behavior is one of the most confused and ill-defined in psychology." A separate volume would be needed to review all of the various definitions and underlying theoretical positions, but a brief outline of the different phenomena considered by those defining emotion will be relevant to issues discussed later.

Some authors have considered central to their definition of emotion a special class of *stimuli* which usually elicit emotional behavior, but there has been little agreement about what might characterize such stimuli or distinguish them from stimuli which rarely elicit emotion. No one has provided a description of the social variables (e.g., the nature of the setting, the roles of the persons, the tasks underway), or the individual differences which might clarify why and when certain classes of stimuli evoke emotional behavior. A further problem is the inability to verify that a stimulus frequently kindles emotion except from the occurrence of consequent emotional behavior; unfortunately, it is equally difficult to verify whether the consequent behavior *is* emotional. There is some agreement, however, that there may be stimuli which elicit emotional behavior because of innate factors, as well as those to which the emotional response is learned; and that, in addition to internal events of the organism, such emotional reactions would also be induced by external or environmental stimuli.

The lack of agreement about what stimuli bring on emotion, and the circularity in the verification of such stimuli, leaves the investigator without guidance in choosing a particular setting or eliciting circumstance which may be likely to inspire emotional facial behavior for study. Thus, when an investigator finds no relationship between some aspect of the face and emotion, there is always the possibility that he failed to utilize stimuli which draw out "emotional" facial behavior.

Physiological responses have been viewed as relevant to some definitions of emotion, including visceral activity, other signs of autonomic activation, and hypothalamic activity. It is generally accepted that the occurrence of such physiological responses is not a sufficient indication of the presence of emotion, and there is little evidence indicating that different emotions are associated with the different patterns of autonomic activity investigated to date.[4]

Some *motor responses* have been considered central to the definition of emotional behavior. Involuntary motor attitudes, voluntary action tendencies, presumed basic patterns of aggression, flight or immobility, and such phenomena as tics and restlessness have been considered. And, of course, the movements of the facial muscles have been regarded by many authors as relevant to or a primary element of emotional behavior. The nature of the relationship between facial behavior and other presumably emotion-related phenomena is the topic of this book.

Certain kinds of *verbal responses* have been part of some definitions of emotion. These would include what Mandler (1962) called referential verbal behavior, descriptions referring to internal somatic states presumably reflecting awareness of physiological activation. They would include, too, the vocabulary of emotion names, categories, dimensions, attributes, or qualities which could be used to describe felt or observed emotional experience.

The *interactive consequence* of certain behavior has been considered by some the necessary criterion for defining emotional behavior. Those investigators of nonhuman primates who speak of emotion define it in terms of a sequence of events between two or more organisms in which a behavior on the part of one is immediately followed by a particular kind of response by another. While some investigators of human nonverbal behavior have begun to study interactive sequences, the only studies of the face which utilized this approach have not been concerned with emotion, and have isolated only one aspect of facial behavior for study, looking or not looking at the face of the other person.

The lack of clarity about what to regard definitive of emotion presents problems not only for investigators (some of whom simply have side-stepped

---

[4] There has been little study of the relationship between facial responses and physiological indices. The few studies compared only one physiological index, GSR, and only a gross measure of the face. (Buck, Savin, Miller, & Caul, 1969; Jones, 1950; Lanzetta & Kleck, 1970); but they found evidence of a negative correlation. A study on the problem is in progress by Ekman, Friesen, and Malmstrom in collaboration with Averill, Opton, and Lazarus which compares GSR, heart rate, and more complex measures of facial behavior.

the problem of specifying just why the behavior they studied may be presumed to have anything to do with emotion), but also for the authors of this volume. How should we determine just which studies are relevant, and how should we utilize this ambiguous concept? Our selection procedure was to take into account, with a few exceptions, any article which the author *said* was about emotion, and where the face was studied in relation to one of the other phenomena listed above. The most common experiment has been to study the face in relation to emotion vocabulary, usually that of the observer, although there have been some studies which have analyzed facial responses under different natural or experimentally arranged environmental conditions. We found no studies of the relationship between referential verbal behavior and facial behavior, although these would have qualified for inclusion, and only a few which included physiological measures.

Studies of the face in which the investigator said he was focusing upon traits, attitudes or personality, not emotion, have not been incorporated. Studies of nonhuman primate facial behavior and most of the literature on the development of human facial behavior have not been considered, because of the recent development of this research and because many of the methodological problems encountered in studying a nonspeaking organism are different from those we will be examining. Also excluded were experiments in which drawings of the face rather than photographs, film, videotape, or live facial behavior were employed; the rationale for this exclusion will be given in Chapter XII.

When we use the word "emotion," in many cases the discussion will apply equally to the various aspects of the term, and therefore there will be no need to specify one. In scrutinizing the results of particular experiments, we will attempt to specify what notion of emotion the investigator had in mind, or at least why he felt the behavior he studied was relevant to emotion. In most studies the behavior investigated was thought to be emotional because observers were able to reach some agreement in utilizing the layman's vocabulary of emotion terms to describe the behavior. When interpretations of results are challenged primarily on grounds of relevance of the behavior studied to emotion, the different sources of evidence (stimuli, motor responses, verbal responses, physiological responses, interactive consequences) will be discussed.

CHAPTER II

How Do We Determine whether Judgments of Emotion Are Accurate?

Can the face provide accurate information about emotion? This simple question, the answer to which may seem patently obvious on an intuitive basis, has baffled investigators. Past reviewers have claimed that the findings from equally reputable investigations are contradictory and that therefore no answer can be proposed. We shall challenge this reading of the literature and, in establishing that the face can provide accurate information, shall criticize in detail and then dismiss as worthless certain experiments; we shall reanalyze and reinterpret others. We will have to consider how investigators solved many of the methodological problems we will be examining in Part Two, and we will need to take careful stock of how they established their criteria of accuracy, for this has been one of the main sources of error and confusion.

If we are to show that the face provides accurate information, we must do two things. Some measurement procedure must be used to decipher the information shown in a face, and some other index of what occurred must be obtained, so that the information from the face can be compared with this index. If they coincide, the face provided accurate information. The accuracy criterion is the index of what occurred; this is compared with the facial information. Part of the confusion in interpreting the past literature has arisen because investigators used different methods to derive their information from the face. Some simply asked observers of the face what emotion was shown, while others have measured some aspect of the face (for example, the lowering or raising of the brows). With either kind of measurement the investigator has the same problem—to find some independent criterion of what occurred to compare with his measurement of information from the face. If,

15

for example, he could ask the person whose face was being measured how he felt at that time, and if he could trust the adequacy and veracity of the person's self-report as his accuracy criterion, he would employ this criterion regardless of which measurement procedure he had used for determining the information shown in the face. If he had asked observers about what the face showed, he could compare their judgment with the person's self-report; or, if he had measured some facial behavior, such as brow lowering, he could determine whether it varied when the person reported different emotions. Thus, a definition of accuracy criteria must allow for the use of either measurement procedure.

We have mentioned one source of information about emotion, the person's self-report, which could be used as an accuracy criterion. Our previous discussion of definitions of emotion showed that there were various events which have been taken to be relevant to emotion (certain stimuli, motor responses, verbal responses, physiological responses, interactive consequences). We will consider these various sources of information as possible accuracy criteria. Further, we will argue for the need to use multiple sources of information.

We will use the term *accuracy* to refer to *"correct" information of some nature being obtained, by some means, from facial behavior.* The criterion for determining what actually did happen, in terms of which to check whether information derived from the face was correct, might be based on one or more of the following phenomena: (1) antecedent events (e.g., the behavior of another interactant, or experimentally introduced, or naturally occurring environmental events); (2) concomitant behavior (e.g., physiological measures, simultaneous verbal behavior, body movements); (3) consequent events (e.g., self-report, motor responses of the person being studied, the other interactant's behavior); (4) consensus by a panel of experts about the individual's experience or behavior.

Few investigators have employed information from more than one such source as their accuracy criterion. Yet, variability across subjects, in their interpretation of similar events or instructions and in their attempts to control rather than show emotion, suggests the wisdom of obtaining multiple indices and combining or comparing them in order to establish accuracy. Each of the possible criteria we have suggested may be incomplete; each may be subject to some sort of error; each may be more useful for one emotion than for another, for one setting than another, for one type of person than another. If these criteria have at least partial independence, in that they are subject to different kinds of error, then as more criteria are employed, alternative explanations based on associated error become less plausible (*see* Campbell & Fiske, 1959).

Our definition of accuracy refers to *correct* information, but does not require that the information be relevant to emotions. To establish that the information derived from the face is correct does not guarantee that the correct information concerns emotion, in any of its various definitions. For example, it may be possible to show that observers are able to distinguish accurately between facial behaviors emitted during the stressful and non-stressful portions of a standardized interview. However, this correct judgment need not necessarily be based on information about emotion; if in the stressful phase the subjects become exhausted, facial cues associated with tiredness could provide the basis for accuracy. The investigator would need other means to show that accurate judgment is relevant to emotional phenomena. He could look at the verbal behavior of the subjects during the stress interviews, or determine if other observers who knew nothing about the interview procedure could agree about judgments utilizing an emotion vocabulary, and whether such judgments would differentiate facial behavior emitted during the nonstressful from that during the stressful parts of the interviews. Or, he might compare the facial behaviors correctly judged with facial behaviors emitted in other situations where there is evidence to presume that emotional behavior occurred.

There is no reason to derogate findings which show accuracy. Correct information from the face is important evidence of the face's ability to provide information about personality, or state of exhaustion, etc.; but it may or may not be related to the construct of emotion. Maintaining the distinction between accurate information from the face and accurate information about emotion is fundamental to resolving some of the confusions in the relationship between the two general research methods for studying the face (Chapter VI), to elucidating problems inherent in the choice of eliciting circumstances (Chapter VII), and to interpreting substantive findings on accuracy (Chapter XV).

Today the construct of "emotion" is still far from validated. Some authors even question the utility of such a construct, suggesting that its only use is as a chapter heading in survey textbooks. Multiple methods and multiple criteria for obtaining accurate information relevant to emotion are, therefore, essential to the pursuit of research in this field. Accuracy obtained with different criteria, all relevant to the different aspects of the phenomena labeled emotional, and relevant to the distinctions among emotions (made either in terms of such categories as anger, fear, sadness, etc., or such dimensions as pleasantness, intensity, control, etc.) is crucial to increasing confidence in the utility of the construct "emotion."

One further part of our definition of accuracy requiring comment is the phrase, "by some means," referring to how correct information is obtained from the face. Shortly, we will discuss two interrelated methods of research, judgment studies and components studies (Chapter VI), one requiring observers to describe the information they derive from facial behavior and the other requiring measurement of some component of facial behavior. Accuracy can be a question in each of these methods, and an accurate finding with one can indicate the probable outcome of the other.

Let us now consider the accuracy criteria which have been employed in studies of the face. The most popular accuracy criterion has been the emotion intended by an actor posing facial behavior. If observers can tell what emotion was posed, or if measurement of the face can show that different facial muscles were involved in different poses, then one type of accuracy is established. The *generality* of such results may be open to question, without diminishing the finding that correct information about the actor's intended emotion can be obtained from the face. Four types of questions about the generality of findings from studies of posing can be raised. Are the findings relevant to spontaneous facial behavior (generality across settings and eliciting circumstances)? Do the results depend upon the few specially gifted actors (generality across persons)? Are the findings attributable to those rare moments when someone emits a decipherable pose (generality across time)? Is exact judgment the privilege of only those who are specially trained as observers (generality across observers)? We will weigh these questions further in the next chapter when we distinguish among these types of generality.

The second basis for an accuracy criterion, employed much less often than actor's intent, is the circumstance in which the facial behavior occurred. If observers can tell what was happening, or if measurements of the face show systematic variations with changing eliciting circumstances, then accuracy is established. One of the problems with this criterion is that it presupposes without substantiation (although there are empirical tests which have rarely been employed) that the same eliciting circumstance evokes the same reaction (emotion?) across persons and, further, if observers are utilized, that the observers know what reaction is likely to occur in each eliciting circumstance. For if the same eliciting circumstance evoked different reactions across persons, or if the circumstance was not thought by observers to elicit a particular reaction, there would be no possibility of achieving accurate results. Even if the situation did elicit the same reaction across subjects, it is necessary to determine whether the subjects were similar in regard to attempts to control or disguise their facial behavior. These problems will be further examined in Chapter IV when we review the control of emotion, and later in the report of Landis' and Coleman's experiments, Chapter XV.

Sometimes observers have been asked to judge the emotion shown in the face rather than the eliciting circumstance, typically with the investigator assuming, but not verifying, that a particular emotion was associated with a particular eliciting circumstance for his stimulus persons. This problem will be further elaborated in Chapter XV.

Even when the accuracy criterion is based upon a spontaneous eliciting circumstance, there are still questions about the generality of the findings. While spontaneous eliciting circumstances have more verisimilitude to real life than does posing, the question still remains as to how general the findings are to real life settings. Further, one must consider whether the stimulus persons and/or the observers were representative or in some way special or unique. And there is a need to establish how often, within the situation studied, facial behavior provided the accurate information. In the next chapter we will discuss these questions about generality.

CHAPTER III

What Does Establishing Generality Entail?

There are four types of questions which can be raised about the generality of the findings from any accuracy study. To establish generality across *eliciting circumstances and settings* one must determine whether the findings in one eliciting circumstance or setting would be valid for another such circumstance or setting. This determination is relevant to studies which employ either posed or spontaneous eliciting circumstances.

This type of generality has been a major source of doubt about accuracy studies involving posed behavior, which some writers have claimed has little generality to spontaneous facial behavior. Even if observers can tell what emotion the poser intended, posing may involve the use of special facial conventions which are irrelevant to the facial behavior occurring when people are engaged in spontaneous behavior. We will scrutinize this argument further when we weigh the choice of eliciting circumstances (Chapter VII), when we report findings on accuracy (Chapter XV), and when we examine cross-cultural studies of posing (Chapter XIX). We will argue that posed facial behavior, while special, is not unique and does have generality to spontaneous facial behavior.

In regard to the use of spontaneous behavior, if a laboratory event is devised, such as a stress interview, the investigator must provide some assessment of the types of real life events to which his laboratory eliciting circumstance is relevant. The stress interview might elicit facial behavior which is accurately judged, but that situation might be fairly unique in the extent of stress induced or in the constraints against retaliation, and have generality only to a limited set of circumstances when people are severely put upon and cannot fight back. Even if a naturally occurring eliciting circumstance is employed, rather than a laboratory event, questions can be raised about generality across settings. For example, it might be possible to derive accurate information from the facial behavior shown during childbirth labor, but there might be few other events in life which evoke such prolonged pain and where the setting permits or encourages uncontrolled facial behavior.

Generality *across persons* refers to whether the findings are general to most people, or just to specially trained persons, such as actors, or just to people with certain personality characteristics, such as extroverts. Generality is severely limited when the posers have been actors, but not when untrained persons pose the emotions. Generality across persons is in doubt in studies of spontaneous behavior if some special group of persons is recruited as subjects, e.g., mental patients.

The third type of generality is *across time* within an eliciting circumstance. How frequently does the face provide true information? In posing, how often does the poser emit facial behavior which is accurately judged; does he give eight poses inaccurately judged for every one judged accurately? In studies of spontaneous facial behavior, has the investigator chosen for his sample the infrequent moment when the face showed something, or does the facial behavior shown in the situation provide precise information at many points in time? The answer to this question about generality depends upon how the investigator sampled facial behaviors from his record, whether of posing or of spontaneous behavior, and will be discussed in Chapter IX. The problem of achieving generality across time will be explored in relation to the spontaneous facial behavior studies which used photographs from magazines as their stimuli, Chapter XV.

The last question on the generality of accuracy findings applies only if observers judge the information shown in the face. Generality of *decoding* asks how readily other observers could make those judgments. Were specially trained or gifted observers used, or was enlargement or slowed motion required for their making exact judgments?

CHAPTER IV

Can Facial Behavior Be Controlled or Disguised?

Many writers (Hebb, 1946; Honkavaara, 1961; Klineberg, 1938; Murphy, Murphy, & Newcomb, 1937; Plutchik, 1962) have commented that a subject's control over his facial behavior and the social pressures which dictate such control can conceal the very behavior the investigator has arranged his experiment to draw out. Ekman and Friesen (1969a, 1969b) have described four management techniques for the control of facial behavior: (1) intensifying, (2) deintensifying, (3) neutralizing, or (4) masking a felt emotion with the facial behavior usually associated with a different emotion. They have hypothesized that these control techniques for managing facial behaviors associated with emotion are operative in most social situations, and that *display rules* are learned, usually early in life, for each facial behavior which specify what management technique should be applied by whom in what circumstances. The display rule dictates the occasion for the applicability of a particular management technique in terms of (a) static characteristics of the persons within the situation (e.g., age, sex, physical body size), (b) static characteristics of the setting (e.g., ecological factors, and social definition of the situation, such as funeral, wedding, job interview, waiting for a bus), (c) transient characteristics of the persons (e.g., role, attitude), and (d) transient regularities during the course of the social interaction (e.g., entrances, exits, transition points, periods in conversation, listening, etc.). Display rules govern facial behavior on an habitual basis, such that they are more noticeable when violated than when followed. The face appears to be the most skilled nonverbal communicator and perhaps for that reason the best "nonverbal liar," capable not only of withholding information but of simulating the facial behavior associated with a feeling which the person in no way is experiencing.

23

In the choice of an eliciting circumstance for sampling nonverbal behavior (Chapter VII), the question of which display rules may be operative for which persons should be considered. Otherwise the investigator may unintentionally obtain samples of deintensified or masked facial behavior. The investigator can utilize questionnaires as well as observations to try to determine the display rules or the social norms about the probable visible facial behavior for the particular eliciting situations he plans to employ. Individual differences in knowledge of display rules or in skill in the management techniques for controlling facial behavior, which might affect the behavior during an experiment, could be explored through self-reports by the subjects about just those questions.

It is not easy for the investigator to determine the effect of display rules, but in the past, investigators have rarely even raised the question of whether their findings might be influenced by, and their negative results attributed to, display rules. Conceivably, there may be circumstances where the display rule specifies that no management technique need be applied to control the facial behavior and unmodulated facial behavior would occur. Most investigators have assumed, with little evidence for that assumption and much reason to question it, that their eliciting situations were those kinds of circumstances.

It is possible, of course, to make the operation of display rules itself the focus of research on the face and emotion. For example, differences in facial behavior could be compared between the subject in isolation and in interaction or aware of being observed. Some such studies are presently in progress, but have not yet been reported.

CHAPTER V

Can Two or More Emotions
Be Shown Simultaneously?

A number of authors (Ekman & Friesen, 1967a, 1969a; Nummenmaa, 1964; Plutchik, 1962; Tomkins & McCarter, 1964) have recently commented on the capacity of the face to show more than one emotion at a given instant. These writers have claimed that the facial muscles are sufficiently complex and independent for discrete muscle patterns in different parts of the face to combine so as to present the elements of two or more emotions, observable even in a still photograph. Blends may also occur through the very rapid succession in time of two different emotions. Affect blends are thought to occur when (a) the emotion-eliciting circumstance by its very nature elicits more than one feeling, or (b) habits (common to a group, or idiosyncratic) link the elicited emotion to another as, for example, when a second emotion is generated in response to the initially inspired one.

Nummenmaa (1964) directly studied this phenomenon by having an actor attempt to show blends in his face. Nummenmaa confirmed that blends could be posed by finding that observers tended to select a blend judgment (e.g., happy and angry) more often than a single affect judgment for the stimuli intended to portray blends, but not for the stimuli intended as single-emotion portrayals. In unpublished research, Ekman and Friesen have found that some of the photographs which past investigators found to yield a bimodal distribution of judgments when observers were allowed only one judgment choice yielded agreement about the presence of both emotions when observers were allowed to indicate the presence of more than one emotion in the face.

Most investigators have failed to take into account the occurrence of blends in their stimuli. The frequent finding that observers disagree about which of two emotions is present can no longer be interpreted only as evidence of low information in the face, but alternatively as the consequence of presenting a multiple message stimulus and allowing the observer only a single message judgment. In other words, low agreement may be a result of the insensitivity of the dependent variable measure to complex forms of facial behavior.

The phenomenon of blends complicates not only the judgment procedure which must be utilized, but also the measures of facial behavior which need to be taken in studies where such measures are related to eliciting circumstances.

REVIEW *Part One: Conceptual Ambiguities*

We discussed five conceptual problems which need to be reviewed in planning or evaluating research on the face and emotion. While no clear agreement about the meaning of the concept *emotion* has yet emerged, consensus suggests that there are some stimuli which typically elicit emotion, that certain physiological, motor, and verbal responses are relevant to emotion, and that there may be specific interactive consequences of emotion. The ambiguity about the meaning of emotion causes problems for the investigator in determining what to study and how to establish that the facial behavior he is observing is relevant to emotion.

The term *accuracy* was defined as referring to correct information of some nature being obtained, by some means, from facial behavior. Four sources of information were described for determining what actually did happen. We argued that multiple sources of information should be used in establishing the criterion of accuracy. We hypothesized that the *control* and disguise of facial behavior are dictated by socially learned display rules which specify how facial behavior is to be managed in particular social settings, by deintensifying, intensifying, neutralizing, or masking the facial behavior associated with an emotion. Investigators must determine whether the eliciting circumstance they have chosen for obtaining facial behavior is subject to display rules which might inhibit or diminish the display of the elicited emotion.

Four kinds of *generality* were considered, which are relevant to findings obtained with posed or spontaneous, artificial or natural eliciting circumstances. Is the finding general to eliciting circumstances and settings other than those studied, and if so to which? Is the finding relevant to the facial behavior of people in general, or only to some special class of persons? Is the finding general to most moments in time within the eliciting circumstance studied, or does the face provide information only occasionally? Finally, in judgment studies, is the finding general to most persons who might observe facial behavior, or does it require some special skills in the observer?

We suggested that the face can probably provide information about *blends* of two or more emotions at a given instant. The existence of blends requires that in judgment studies observers be given the option of reporting an impression about more than one emotion. In studies where measurement is made of facial components, it is necessary to examine various areas of the face in order to determine whether a particular facial behavior is relevant to one or more than one emotion.

In Part Two we will discuss how these conceptual issues translate into specific methodological decisions which must be made in planning research on the face and emotion.

PART TWO

Methodological Decisions

We will take into consideration each of the decisions an investigator confronts in planning research on the face and emotion. The choices which have been made in the past will be evaluated and a recommendation will be made regarding each methodological decision. While the chief aim of these chapters is to provide some guidelines for those planning research on facial behavior, these discussions of problems encountered in trying to do research on the face provide the critical framework which we will be applying in Part Three when we review and evaluate the research findings on each of seven substantive questions.

CHAPTER VI

Selecting a Research Design

One source of confusion in research on the face and emotion has been an oversimplification of the relationship between results obtained from two separate research approaches which address related but not identical questions. In *component studies*, facial behavior is treated as a response, and the question addressed is whether a certain position or movement of the subject's face is related to some measure of the subject's emotional state or circumstances. For example, do the inner corners of the eyebrows lift when the subject reports or simulates sadness? In *judgment studies*, facial behavior is treated as a stimulus, and the question addressed is whether observers who judge a subject's face can agree about the subject's emotion or can distinguish between facial behaviors emitted under different emotional states or circumstances. For example, can observers correctly distinguish facial behaviors emitted when the subject reports or simulates happiness from those reflected when he reports or simulates sadness? While in the natural flow of social interaction the faces of the participants provide both stimuli and responses, in most research one or the other aspect has been studied, and with quite different methods.

Judgment studies have been much more popular than component studies throughout the history of research. This has been due only partly to the impression that they are easier to perform, in that the investigator can avoid the problem of what to measure in the face and must decide only what faces to show and what judgments to require. In addition, the attraction of judgment studies has been in the possibility of answering both judgment and component questions with one study. The investigator has attempted not only to discover whether observers can judge emotion, but also to infer from that result whether components of facial behavior are related to eliciting circumstances. Most investigators have failed to understand that the answer to the components question can be inferred only when the answers to the

31

judgment study are accurate, not when they show inaccuracy or disagreement among judges.

If a judgment study finds that the observers were accurate, then it can be inferred that a component study of the same facial behavior would find that the faces varied with the eliciting circumstance. This relationship between the outcomes of these two research approaches is logically required, since observers would not have any basis for making accurate judgments if the facial behavior did not vary with the eliciting circumstance. But a judgment study may not be successful; the observers may disagree, or they may agree but be inaccurate rather than accurate. If either of these unfortunate outcomes occurs, it is not logically possible to determine what is at fault. Typically, investigators who have failed to obtain accuracy in judgment studies have concluded that the faces they studied must not contain information relevant to the accuracy criterion, and that if a component study were performed, no relationship would be found between facial behavior and eliciting circumstances. But this is not logically necessary. When a judgment study fails, the information *may* have been there in the face, and it *might* be unearthed by a component study, if for some reason the observers failed to utilize the information which was there. Observers might miss the clues if they do not know what components of facial behavior are related to a particular eliciting circumstance, or if they have mistaken notions of how the components relate to the eliciting circumstance, of if an atypical sample of facial behavior was selected for showing to the observers, or if there was an atypical sampling of observers, or if the facial behaviors are difficult to see without slowed motion viewing.

Recent, still tentative findings (Ekman & Friesen, 1969a; Haggard & Isaacs, 1966) on micro affect displays suggest that a failure of observers to agree (or, if they agree, to be accurate) may signify not that the facial behaviors are unrelated to the eliciting circumstances, but that they are too brief for the observers to perceive. Micro affect displays have been defined as facial behaviors of so short a duration that most untrained observers do not notice their occurrence, even though inspection of slow motion film reveals behaviors associated with emotion which observers can readily judge. Such micro facial behaviors may be indicators of conflict, repression, and/or efforts to conceal the emotion experienced.

Thus, if a judgment study fails to yield accuracy, the investigator must be cautious about inferring that the facial behavior is unrelated to the eliciting circumstances. While that might be so, it is just as possible that the observers' failure was due to one of the problems we have mentioned briefly, and which we will explore at greater length in the next six chapters.

In this examination of the relationship between these two methods of research, judgment studies and component studies, we have avoided the term *emotion* when speaking of accuracy. It could well be that observers can correctly judge a poser's *intention* to show a particular emotion, and thus we could infer that some of the components of the facial behaviors emitted when posing the different emotions were different. And yet, such a finding would not in and of itself be evidence that the observers recognized emotion. A variety of behaviors (i.e., lip bites, hesitations, sighs, refusals) might have occurred in reaction to a particular posing instruction, and thus allowed accurate judgment. Similarly, if the investigator had arranged eliciting circumstances such that the subject was given a severe electric shock on his leg in one circumstance and not in another, it might well be that observers told of the circumstances would correctly identify the facial behavior which occurred in each, and might also judge the electric shock behavior as fear, and the nonshock facial behavior as happiness. Such a finding would logically require the inference that some of the components of the facial behavior were related to the eliciting circumstance. But we cannot assume that the accuracy necessarily involved emotional phenomena. Analysis of the facial components shown in that situation could reveal that during shock the subject bent down to look at his leg, completely obscuring his face, while in nonshock he looked straight into the camera. There certainly would be a difference in facial behavior related to eliciting circumstance, and a ready explanation of the observer's accuracy, but it would be rather poor evidence for asserting that the face provided accurate information about emotion. This is admittedly an extreme example, intended to emphasize the necessity for the investigator to demonstrate that his accuracy findings, whether from a component study or a judgment study, have sufficient relevance to phenomena described as emotional to warrant the use of that term.

CHAPTER VII

Choosing the Eliciting Circumstance

Three requirements must be met in the choice of circumstances during which facial behavior is sampled. (1) There should be some basis for claiming the circumstance has relevance to emotion. (2) There should be some way to determine when emotion was aroused or simulated, and, if possible, which emotion was aroused or simulated when, so as to provide an accuracy criterion for use in either component or judgment studies. (3) A clear record must be obtained if the crucial components are to be either measurable or evident to observers. The two alternatives, posed and spontaneous situations, each satisfy only one of the first two requirements and each has potential liabilities where the other has strength. Posing provides clearer indications than do spontaneous situations of *which* (intended) emotion is shown *when*. Spontaneous situations can claim to have greater relevance than posing to more usual emotional circumstances.

Posing is easy to arrange; clear records are readily obtained; and the record is composed of separate units identified in terms of specific emotions according to the poser's intent. But there are problems. Although posing may differ from other situations in terms of the relative absence of display rules to deintensify, neutralize, or mask facial behavior, posers may well differ in their ability to simulate given emotions, and the typical study has unfortunately used only one or two posers. While the actor may intend to show only one emotion, posed behavior may contain blends of intended and unintended simulated emotions. Another difficulty is that of choosing which poses to consider, since most actors will not achieve a pose acceptable to them or the investigator on every attempt; this problem will be taken up later in regard to sampling of behaviors.

The most serious question about posing, raised throughout the history of research on the face and emotion, is whether posed facial behavior has relevance to spontaneously occurring emotion. Hunt (1941) was the most forceful spokesman for the view that posed facial behavior is a specialized, conventionalized language which, while related to emotion words, is unrelated to the facial behavior occurring when emotion is spontaneously experienced. Thus, positive findings on the judgment of poses were not considered by Hunt to challenge his conclusion that spontaneous facial behavior, when emotion is aroused, is a meager source of information, if not a random phenomenon. But that view depends upon argument, not direct evidence, and recent findings suggest its opposite.

Only two investigators directly compared posed and spontaneous facial behavior from the same subjects: Coleman (1949) in a judgment study, and Landis (1924, 1929), in both a judgment and a component study. Unfortunately, few conclusions can be derived from their work. Coleman used only two subjects, and the relationship between posed and spontaneous behavior differed for each. Landis' studies are open to criticism on a wide variety of grounds which will be examined later. Recent cross-cultural studies which have found that the same posed facial behavior was judged as showing the same emotion across various cultures and languages, including a preliterate culture, offer indirect evidence against Hunt's view. If posed facial behavior were an arbitrary language, it would be highly improbable that the same poses would develop in the same way and be associated with comparable verbal labels across cultures (*see* pages 105–106, 166–167 for discussion of these findings).

Nevertheless, it would be important to have both judgment and component studies directed to this question, to examine the differences and similarities between posed and spontaneous facial behavior on the same set of subjects. Such studies would be useful because of the history of frequent use of the posing method and the need to answer more decisively Hunt's criticism. In addition, judgment studies could determine whether observers can distinguish felt (spontaneous) emotion from simulated (posed) emotion, and component studies could lead to greater understanding of simulated or deceptive facial behavior as it occurs in spontaneous social interactions. Later (Chapter XV), when we review experiments on the accuracy of judgments of the poser's intentions, we will again consider the relationship between posed and spontaneous behavior, and suggest some hypotheses about their similarities and differences.

Spontaneous eliciting circumstances have been presumed to be more relevant to emotion, although it may be more difficult to record the behavior, and specification of *what* emotion is shown *when* may be impossible or possible only in gross terms. The most frequently used spontaneous circumstance (e.g., by Coleman, Dunlap, Landis, Lanzetta, and Kleck) has been the experimentally arranged, emotion-evoking event—electric shock, tickling, etc. The record is segmented, with a different emotion presumed to be induced in each of the evocation episodes, and the episode, or the emotion, presumed to be elicited in it, serves as the accuracy criterion. As discussed earlier (pages 18–24), there are problems with this type of procedure. The event arranged by the experimenter may or may not evoke an emotion and the event may or may not, for most or some subjects, lead to inhibiting or disguising the facial behavior. In some experiments the self-reports of subjects have shown variability in whether they experienced emotion and, if so, which emotion, but these data were usually disregarded. Given the ambiguous status of the concept of emotion stimuli, some attempt should be made to assess, independently of the face, whether the experimentally-arranged situation normally is associated with any emotion, and whether it is associated with emotion for the subjects in the study.

Remarkably little use has been made of naturally occurring, spontaneous situations. The exception is the use of magazine photographs of presumably emotional events (Hanawalt, Munn, Vinacke). In these studies, the investigators did not specify how they decided a situation was relevant to emotion, nor did they make any attempt to verify independently whether the situations they selected are normatively associated with emotions. And selecting photographs from magazines deprives the investigator of any knowledge of representativeness of the behavior shown in the stimulus, leading to doubts about the generality of the results (*see* pages 90–94).

A few investigators have looked at naturally occurring or experimentally arranged interactions where there is independent evidence that emotion occurs, but their studies suffer from their inability to make more than a gross distinction between positive and negative emotion (*see* pages 95–102).

It should be noted that the distinction between posed and spontaneous behavior is not directly parallel to the distinction between artificial and natural occurrences. Though posing is by definition artificial (perhaps having only remote resemblance to the simulation of emotion naturally occurring during conversations), spontaneous behavior may or may not be natural. Spontaneous behavior is natural when some part of life itself leads to the behavior which is studied. Spontaneous behavior elicited in the laboratory may be representative of some naturally occurring spontaneous behavior, or conceivably it could be artificial if the eliciting circumstance is quite unique and not relevant to any known real life event. The investigator must be concerned with demonstrating that results gathered in the laboratory have relevance (generality) to some type of naturally occurring facial behavior.

The difficulty in many studies utilizing spontaneous laboratory situations has not been a lack of relevance to real life but a failure to appreciate what aspect of life has been represented in the laboratory. For example, telling the subject a joke or shocking him may be most relevant to nonlaboratory situations where the person disguises or conceals his emotional reaction from authoritative figures, rather than being representative of how the person shows his emotions with his friends. If the investigator chooses to study naturally occurring, spontaneous facial behavior he avoids the problem of demonstrating relevance to actual life, but usually at the cost of greatly increasing his difficulties in recording the phenomena and specifying what emotion has occurred when.

Some standards can be listed as guides:

1. Experimenters should select more than one eliciting circumstance. If only posing is used, then posing under different instructions, or posing, role-playing, acting, etc., could be used to avoid the hazard that peculiarities in one way of eliciting the pose will bias the sample. If only spontaneous situations are used, then there should be quite a variety of such situations—for example, when an individual is alone, when the investigator is present, when the emotion is aroused by a noxious event, a film, an action of another person, etc.

2. Some attempt should be made to assess whether the situation was associated with a particular emotion for subjects in general as well as for the particular subjects studied. With posing, the poser's impression as to whether he managed to show the intended emotion on each trial would be useful. In spontaneous situations, simultaneous or retrospective self-reports could be gathered about felt emotion, and the emotion-provoking situations could be judged by other groups of subjects in terms of whether they would expect a particular emotion in that situation and whether they would expect display rules to be operative.

3. If the investigator uses an artificial eliciting circumstance (either posing or experimentally elicited emotions), he must provide some estimation of the relevance of his findings to naturally occurring emotions.

CHAPTER VIII

Sampling Persons

Bruner and Tagiuri (1954) emphasized the need for representative sampling of persons whose facial behavior is recorded, in order to avoid error due to either morphological characteristics or differing ability to show certain emotions. In our terms, such sampling of persons is crucial if the results from either component or judgment studies are not to be unduly biased by the habitual emotion blends or the idiosyncratic application of display rules by a particular person. Since Bruner and Tagiuri's review, the size of the sample of stimulus persons in judgment studies has generally been far greater than before (although some investigators have persisted in publishing on judgments made of one actor's poses), which may in part explain the better results recently obtained.

While inadequate sampling of persons could bias results and limit the generality of findings, individual or group differences in facial behavior could also be a substantive issue. Tomkins and McCarter (1964) hypothesized personality variables which might account for differences in ability to emit emotions, but the one study on this topic (Levitt, 1964) did not reveal correlates of the substantial differences among posers in their ability to show facial behaviors which observers could understand. Other investigators have also sought correlates of individual differences in posing ability, with little success to date, but some promise for the future.

The standard here is a simple one. Studies which employ many subjects are more trustworthy than those which use only a few. A more complex formulation of this standard is that the more subjects for which the eliciting circumstance succeeded in evoking the intended response, the sounder the study.

CHAPTER IX

Sampling Behavior from a Record

Usually only a part of a permanent record of facial behavior can be either shown to observers in a judgment study or measured in a component study. Sampling is necessary, often because there is just too much material to analyze, sometimes because a record contains a number of episodes in which the eliciting circumstance obviously backfired or the subject failed. For example, not every person may be able to pose every emotion on every attempt; or, a presumed humorous situation may just not be funny for anyone or everyone. There is nothing sacrosanct about eliciting circumstances which would argue against sampling only some of the facial behavior which was recorded, unless the circumstance itself is the primary object of study. When the eliciting circumstance is not the object of study, but the means for gathering records of facial behavior, quite selective sampling is permissible.

Investigators have typically sampled the behavior they thought was "best" without stating the basis of their choices, or the amount of behavior and number of subjects excluded. Without such information, it is impossible to determine the generality of their findings across persons, or settings, or over time within the circumstance they studied; and uncertainty about generality has created unwarranted suspicion about their substantive findings as well. But, if the question addressed is, for example, whether observers *can* be accurate in their judgments, or whether the movements of the eyebrows are *ever* related to fear-arousing stimuli, sampling which may restrict generality does not invalidate the findings. Unless the sampling procedures have been specified, the related question of *how often* the face provides accurate information (for what kinds of persons, observers, emotions, circumstances, etc.) cannot be answered.

A number of specific bases for sampling can be developed which will allow determination of generality and comparison with findings from replications.

41

Extensive pretesting could provide the basis for evaluating particular instructions, eliciting circumstances, or even types of subjects. For example, pretesting a set of instructions for posing, by having subjects use a multidimensional rating instrument to record the emotion they would try to display, might reveal that certain instructions tend to induce an affect blend rather than a single affect; such instructions could be discarded or modified. Describing an eliciting circumstance or showing it on film and having subjects describe the emotion they would expect to experience might reveal that a particular eliciting circumstance does not evoke the particular emotion the investigator had expected, and it could be modified. Pretesting subjects might show that certain people are generally embarrassed in a posing situation and will not provide variable facial behavior. If the demographic, attitudinal and/or personality characteristics of such people were determined, others who share those characteristics could be excluded as stimulus persons or the results treated separately. All of these procedures would eliminate, before records are collected, the likelihood of obtaining facial behavior which would not be relevant to the purposes of the experiment. The investigator would avoid the procedure of subjectively picking his best stimulus persons, as has often been the case in studies of both spontaneous and posed behavior. Instead, he could draw a representative sample from his records, and specify the basis for excluding stimulus persons or eliciting circumstances, so that the generality of his findings across persons, circumstances, and over time within the situation would be known.

This same objective can also be reached by obtaining other sources of information at the time records are collected. For example, posers could be asked to describe whether or not they think they responded with a good pose for each pose attempted; or subjects in a stress interview could listen to the interview afterwards and indicate the points at which they were maximally uncomfortable; or galvanic skin conductance records during a stress interview could be consulted for the points of maximal arousal. Again, the investigator would not be forced to sample subjectively, but could specify the basis for his sampling, thus providing the relevant data for evaluating the generality of his findings.

It is least preferable to utilize the appearance of the facial behavior itself as the basis for sampling. If the investigator does this, he should specify the principle underlying his selection of the "good" faces, furnishing information also about the number of rejected faces.

The standard in regard to sampling of behavior from a record is that the investigator should specify how this was done so that generality of findings can be determined.

CHAPTER X

Sampling Emotions

Over- or under-representation of some emotions within the sample of facial behavior may seriously bias the outcome of either a judgment or a component study. Almost all of the empirical research has shown that happiness is most easily recognized and distinguished from other emotions, and this result seems to obtain across a number of cultures and languages (*see* page 157, Table 13). Although the evidence is not yet as firm, it would appear that some discriminations among emotions, whether made by an observer or by some measurement of facial components, are more difficult than others. Fear and surprise, for example, are probably more similar to each other in both facial components and semantic connotations than either is with disgust. Very different findings on judgment agreement, accuracy, components, or judgment of underlying dimensions of emotion may occur because experimenters have differently sampled emotions. An example of this problem is a study by Abelson and Sermat (1962) which analyzed dissimilarity ratings of observers on a sample of faces in order to determine the dimensions which might underlie judgments of emotion. We checked the previously published norms on the facial stimuli they utilized and found their selection very skewed: six *fear* and four *happiness* pictures, only one *anger*, one *contempt*, one *disgust*, and no *surprise*.

As discussed earlier, the lack of agreement among theorists about emotion and the names of emotions makes it difficult for the investigator to know what emotions should be included in his sample of facial behavior if it is to be representative. Almost all of the procedures discussed in Chapter IX, "Sampling Behavior from a Record," can also be utilized to ascertain what emotions may be represented within a sample of facial behavior; and the results from a judgment study can also be examined for this purpose. In our discussion of findings about the categories and dimensions of emotion (*see*

Chapters XIII and XIV), we will show that there are some consistencies across studies to help an investigator ensure that his sample includes at least those which have been commonly found by others.

The standard regarding this problem is that the investigator should provide information about what emotions have been sampled in his study. The more emotions sampled, the greater the generality.   In data analysis, results should be presented so that it is possible to determine how many of the findings can be attributed to the straightforward discrimination of *happiness* from everything else. Preferably, results should be reported in terms of each emotion or dimension, or each circumstance sampled.

CHAPTER XI

Sampling Emotion Words, Categories, or Dimensions in Judgment Studies

In a judgment study, the observer must record his decision about the emotion shown in a face by utilizing either a restricted set of terms provided by the investigator or his own words. Although in a few experiments the observer did not utilize emotion vocabularies (at least in ways known to the investigator), but instead grouped photographs (e.g., Hulin & Katz, 1935), interpretation of the results has been difficult; the basis for grouping or of similarity ratings between pairs of stimuli has not usually been made explicit, and no study has allowed a direct comparison between the results of this method and the more usual judgment task.

Free responses in the observer's own words have been less popular in recent years, perhaps because of Woodworth's finding that organizing such free responses into categories yielded considerably higher agreement and accuracy (*see* pages 58–60). Yet restricting the observer's choice to a preselected list seriously limits the import of the results, *if* the purpose of the study is to determine the nature of the emotion vocabulary, or to check some formulation about the basic or primary emotion categories or the underlying dimensions of emotion. While such a study can reveal the differential applicability of any set of preselected terms, it cannot indicate whether more categories or dimensions might have been found if the investigator had not limited the observer's choices.

A commonly applied solution to this problem has been unsatisfactory because of inadequate sampling of stimuli. In a number of experiments, the vocabulary given observers was based upon the words provided most frequently by another set of observers who had been allowed to select their own words when looking at a set of facial stimuli. If, as has usually been the case, the facial stimuli consisted of the behavior of just one or two persons, with no evidence that emotions were representatively sampled, then the verbal list derived from the most frequent words may be quite limited, and the findings cannot claim generality about the nature of the emotion vocabulary to more than the particular pictures judged.

There are, however, many experiments in which the focus of the study justifies the use of a preselected emotion vocabulary in the judgment task. When the aim of the study is *not* to determine comprehensive answers to questions about the nature of the emotion vocabulary or judgment procedure applicable to facial behavior, the use of preselected lists of words, categories, or dimensions may be the most economical procedure in both observer time and subsequent data analysis. If the purpose of the study is to measure differences in accuracy depending, let us say, upon whether the eye area or mouth area is observed, a preselected list of emotion categories or scales is an appropriate judgment procedure. However, the investigator must be aware that different results might have been obtained if other emotion choices had been given to the observers, and his results will be more credible if he shows that his preselected emotion terminology is sufficiently comprehensive for the purposes of his study.

A last problem in connection with judgment procedure was taken under consideration earlier in regard to the phenomenon of emotion blends (*see* Chapter V). Although the evidence is still tentative, it appears likely that even still photographs of the face may frequently contain components of more than one emotion, and that observers may well be able to determine the presence of particular combinations or blends if the investigator allows them to do so. If the stimulus does contain an emotion blend, and the investigator allows only a single choice from a preselected list which does not contain blend terms, then spuriously low levels of agreement may result, since some of the observers may choose a term for one of the blend components, some for another. There are a number of judgment procedures which could be utilized to allow observers to indicate the presence of blends, and the particular emotions involved in a blend. The problem, of course, is less severe if observers are allowed to use their own words (and more than one), but then the investigator must, in his data analysis, be sensitive to the possibility of blend responses in perhaps differing words.

There are two standards. Attention to the question of representative sampling of emotion terms, inclusion of more rather than fewer terms, and, at some stage of the research, allowance for free responses would be desirable in most judgment experiments and crucial in those which have as their purpose a determination about the nature of the emotion vocabulary applicable to judgments of the face. Second, some provision should be made for the possibility that the stimuli may contain emotion blends, by providing some means for the observers to indicate their perception of more than one emotion if such is the case.

CHAPTER XII

Choosing a Method of Recording

There has been some argument over the relative merit of motion (film or videotape) and still (photographs) records of facial behavior. An influential opinion has been that of Bruner and Tagiuri (1954), who decried the use of still photographs because "judgment based on a frozen millisecond of exposure" is not representative of the type of judgment made in naturally occurring conditions. If, however, the purpose of the study does not require a judgment of sequential behavior, then still photographs may be useful for some research questions.

Stills may be appropriate when the information obtainable from the muscle actions at the apex of a facial movement is of interest, rather than information derived from such time variables as latency, duration, and different rates of onset and decay from different facial muscles. But still photographs may lead to judgments or measures which include information based upon permanent physiognomic features rather than transient muscle movements, if only one picture of a stimulus person is shown; without a baseline, permanent facial wrinkles may not be distinguishable from wrinkles caused by a particular muscle contraction. Nevertheless, the savings in cost and ease of use may justify the use of stills in studies of posed facial behavior, where the poser holds the pose for the camera; a still will provide the same information as five seconds of film or videotape of the frozen position. Certainly, there is considerable evidence that the frozen few milliseconds of a still photograph *can* provide quite a bit of information.

In spontaneous eliciting circumstances, however, still photographs may mutilate the natural flow of behavior into meaningless units, particularly if the photographs are taken arbitrarily in disregard of the natural flow of events and the timing of changes in facial behavior. Motion picture film or videotape must be used in such situations, and when the aforementioned time variables are to be studied.

There have been only three experiments which compared observers' judgments made on the basis of a motion picture film record with those made from selected still frames from the same record. Dusenbury and Knower (1938) found that observers who had seen the motion picture film were more accurate in identifying the posed emotion of two stimulus persons than were those who had seen a selected still frame, although even the latter achieved an accuracy level far better than chance. Frijda (1953) obtained the same result, but his eliciting circumstance included elements of posing as well as spontaneous situations, and his scoring procedure for determining the accuracy of the observer's judgment was admittedly subjective. Kozel and Gitter (1968) found that observers were more accurate in judging the intended emotions of ten professional actresses in a silent motion picture film, compared to selected still frames for anger, surprise and fear, but there was no difference in accuracy between the observers who saw motion picture film and still photographs for the poses of happiness, disgust, and sadness. A significant level of accuracy was obtained by the observers who saw the still photographs for all the emotions. Thus, the evidence suggests that still photographs may not be as adequate a method for presenting posed facial behavior as motion picture film, but this stilted recording procedure does present sufficient information for accurate judgments of static events.

Some experiments have not used a permanent record, either motion or still, but instead have had the actor pose live in front of the audience of observers. There are a number of problems with this procedure. Replication with the same stimuli is not possible; control over the stimulus input to the observers is difficult; and at least one investigator noted that extraneous behaviors (e.g., blushing or refusing to pose "love") contributed to accuracy. Feedback from the observers as to whether or not they seem to be getting the message can lead the poser to vary his performance and to utilize behaviors other than the facial behaviors which might ordinarily be associated with emotions.

The last technique of recording facial behavior, which was quite popular in the early years of research, is to rely upon artists' drawings. While drawings have the virtue of allowing control over demographic characteristics, lighting, and various physiognomic features, they have the enormous failing that they may include as facial behavior components which simply do not occur or cannot co-occur, and possible idiosyncratic or stereotypic views of the artist. Until a systematic means of scoring facial behaviors has been widely accepted and drawings as well as large numbers of actual photographs and films have been scored, there is no way of knowing to what extent the drawings represent

fantasy or reality. Considering, for example, a drawing of the face when the lips are drawn back, it is not possible to know how many behaviors which usually occur have been left out, how many "behaviors" have been added in that area of the face which cannot occur with that movement, and how many facial features have been added which just do not occur at all. We have for this reason not considered[5] any of the research in which drawings were used, such as experiments which used the Piderit faces, the Rudolf faces (drawings presumably from photographs but retouched and having the additional problem of a thick beard and moustache covering the lower part of the face), and more recent studies using simple moon-type cartoon faces which reduce facial behavior to a few curved lines.[6]

The standard is that the recording technique be appropriate to the eliciting circumstance and the type of facial behavior under study. Motion records are preferable to stills for most purposes, but either is preferable to live, non-permanent records.

---

[5] It is interesting to note that most of the studies of the face which have produced negative results have been studies of some artistic analog to the face rather than studies which have used a record of actual behavior. See Chapter XV.

[6] The use of drawings of the face, even highly simplified ones, might provide some leads to understanding which facial components are relevant to the judgment of which emotions. This question will be discussed in Chapter XVI, and we have included one study which did utilize drawings of the face for this purpose.

REVIEW *Part Two: Methodological Decisions*

We began by distinguishing two research approaches to the study of the face and emotion, a *component* study and a *judgment* study. We emphasized that failure to find that the observers made accurate judgments or agreed in their judgments does not necessarily signify that the facial components are unrelated to the eliciting circumstances. Certainly, that is one explanation of a failure in a judgment study—the facial behavior was meaningless, and would be shown to be so if measurements of the components were taken. But negative results in a judgment study could also be due to defects in the judgment task, in the sampling of observers, in the sampling of facial behavior, in the recording procedures employed, or in the sampling of persons. All of these considerations apply also to the design of component studies, with the exception of the sampling of words used in a judgment task.

In reviewing the literature in the next chapters, we shall see that there have been relatively few component studies, probably because judgment studies are much easier to perform, and because determining how to measure facial components is a complex problem. This paucity of component studies may change now that there are three new systems for measuring facial components (*see* Chapter XVI). Knowledge would be best advanced by research strategies which combined the use of both component and judgment approaches to the same facial behavior. Then it would be possible to determine how much information the observer can interpret, what facial components relate to his inferences about emotion, and what facial behaviors systematically vary with emotion but are not recognized or consistently interpreted by observers.

We have described guidelines regarding each of the methodological decisions the investigator must make in planning his research, which will also be useful as standards in evaluating the past research literature. We argued that investigators should utilize more than one *eliciting circumstance* from which to draw the facial behavior they intend to study, and they should obtain some evidence that their eliciting circumstance was associated with a particular emotion(s) for their subjects. The standard in regard to the *sampling of persons* was that there should be more than a few stimulus persons, in order to rule out bias due to idiosyncracies in facial behavior. In *sampling behaviors from a record*, we recommended a number of procedures to give the investigator a basis other than his own intuition for selecting faces from his records for study. Information about the sampling procedures he follows is necessary if the generality of his findings is not to be in doubt. The investigator should also specify the emotions he has sampled in his study, and present his data for evaluation of whether his results can be reduced to the simple distinction between positive and negative emotions, or whether he has succeeded in making finer discriminations. In judgment studies, we argued that the investigator should at least include the *emotion terms* and scales which have been consistently found by others, and preferably he should allow free verbal response by his observers at some stage in his study. Provision should also be made for observers to indicate a judgment of affect blends. We argued that motion records (film or video) are preferable to still photographs, although stills are appropriate for such frozen events as poses. Neither live non-permanent records nor drawings from imagination are useful *recording techniques*.

No single experiment should be expected to meet fully every one of the standards we have described. The importance of a particular standard will depend upon the particular study at issue. In the following chapters where research findings are considered, we will emphasize some methodological standards more than others when examining each substantive question.

PART THREE

Research Findings

In the following chapters, we will integrate findings from many different experiments to review and, where possible, to resolve seven major questions about the face and emotion. We have not attempted to include every experiment relevant to every question discussed, but only those which have been influential, those which have been misinterpreted, those which deserve more attention than they have received, and those which clarify fundamental issues or raise important new questions. In order to clarify some of the contradictory results about some of the questions, it was necessary to evaluate each group of experiments in terms of the methodological standards we explored in previous chapters. Studies which did not report their methods in sufficient detail to permit such an evaluation were usually excluded if their findings did not contradict the interpretation we suggest. It was also necessary to reanalyze or to recast results from different experiments if consistencies were to be revealed. Studies which did not report their data in a way which allowed such a reanalysis were excluded if other studies with similar findings could be used instead. For reasons described earlier (pages 50–51) almost all of the studies which used drawings of the face were also excluded.

No claim can be made that the seven substantive questions to be considered are the only basic ones, but they certainly have been the most frequently raised in past studies and again in the current crop of articles. By focusing attention on these, in some cases bringing together evidence to indicate that the questions have been answered, and in other instances indicating where further evidence is now needed, we hope to provide some sense of the state of the field and the most fruitful direction for future research.

In the subsequent chapters, we have utilized tables as the primary means of reporting information about experiments. We *urge* the reader to consider, not skip, the tables. We have usually not summarized in the text material which is described in the tables. Our discussion will always presume familiarity with material shown there.

CHAPTER XIII

What Emotion Categories
Can Observers Judge
from Facial Behavior ?

Most investigators, regardless of the particular question they have asked, have employed a judgment rather than a component study, requiring observers to use some kind of emotion vocabulary and judgment procedure to identify the emotions they perceive. Two judgment procedures have been used, an emotion *category* task in which the observer selects one category, or sometimes two categories, for each example of facial behavior, and a *dimension* task in which the observer rates each face on a series of scales. These two judgment procedures represent and have been utilized to study two distinct theoretical viewpoints about the emotional information which can be obtained from the face.

Some theorists have postulated a set of basic emotion categories, or primary affects. Each of these categories includes a set of words denoting related emotions which may differ in intensity, degree of control, or, in minor ways, in denotative meaning. While the principle of inclusion is not always explained, the words within a category are held to be more similar than the words across categories. Presumably different facial behaviors are associated with each of these emotion categories, although no theorist has ever fully explicated the exact nature of such differences in facial components. Some category theorists have further hypothesized interrelationships among all or some of their emotion categories, which allow representation of their categories within a geometric model, and a delineation of certain dimensions which differentiate among the categories.

The dimension theorists have been most interested in such scales or dimensions which they postulate best describe and underlie (again, in a manner usually unspecified) the emotion categories. Dimension theorists have formulated a small set of independent dimensions, smaller in almost all cases than the number of primary emotion categories proposed by the category theorists, which best describe the differences among facial behaviors associated with emotion and, further, are relevant to describing emotional phenomena other than facial behavior.

Judgments of the face have been used by some to test, at least in part, their theory of categories or dimensions, and by others to derive empirically some proposed set of categories or dimensions. In this chapter, we will consider the evidence on categories of emotion, and in the next chapter we will turn to studies of emotion dimensions.

Research on this question extends over thirty years from Woodworth's (1938) to Frijda's current studies (1968a, 1968b). Actually, the first experimental investigator to propose a set of emotion categories was F. Allport in 1924. The choices made in sampling stimulus persons and emotions from differing eliciting circumstances, and with observers allowed to utilize a wide variety of emotion words in making their judgment, are the most crucial for a decisive answer to this question. Table 1 lists these and other methodological decisions for the five investigators who focused upon the question of what emotion categories can be judged from facial behavior.

Inspection of Table 1 shows that each experiment had serious methodological deficiencies. Only posed behavior has been utilized as the eliciting circumstance. Most studies used only one or two stimulus persons; while Osgood had fifty people pose, he had each emotion posed by only five people, thus allowing, as did the other investigators, the possibility that idiosyncracies of a few people could bias the results. Even Tomkins and McCarter's 11 persons do not represent a sufficient sampling of persons. Most experimenters presented as stimuli only the handful of emotions which they believed to be relevant to their theoretical formulation; Osgood is a noteworthy exception, presenting 40 different emotion poses. None of the studies permitted free responses by the observers, although both Osgood and Frijda did the next best thing by including many words, rather than limiting the observers' choice to prescribed emotion category labels. Their evidence deserves more weight than that from the other investigations, because instead of showing that observers could agree in their use of a preselected set of emotion categories, Osgood and Frijda both showed that a set of categories emerged from the judges' use of the larger list of words they were given. None of the investigators used motion picture film or videotape; Osgood used live behavior but, for reasons discussed earlier (*see* page 50), live behavior raises the possibility of other sources of error.

TABLE 1

Methodological Considerations Regarding Studies of Emotion Categories

	Woodworth 1938	Plutchik 1962	Tomkins & McCarter 1964	Osgood 1966	Frijda 1968b
1. Number of Different Stimulus Persons	1	2	11	50 or 5***	2
2. Number of Different Emotions Posed	10	*	8	40	Not Reported
3. Number of Stimuli	19	26	69	200	130
4. Number of Emotion Words or Categories Given the Observers	10	8	8	40	100
5. Method of Deriving Emotion Words or Categories	Most Frequent when Given List of 107 Words	Theory	Theory	Past Literature	Not Reported
6. Eliciting Circumstance	Pose	*	Pose	Pose	Pose
7. Recording Technique	Still	Still	Still	Live	Still
8. Evidence for Author's Categories	Correlation Poser's Intent and Observer's Judgment	**	Observer Agreement	Cluster Analysis and Factor Analysis	Factor Analysis

 * Had actor attempt to move each facial muscle in all possible ways, rather than pose emotions.
 ** Ratings of words separately, judgments of parts of the face, combining partial faces into total face, and then naming the emotion shown.
 *** See explanation in the text.

While these methodological problems raise doubts about the findings of each experiment if it is considered singly, some of these problems can be remedied by considering the findings across all five studies. If we credit only those results which were consistent across experiments, they derive from a sufficient sampling of stimulus persons, emotions, stimuli and emotion words. (The only limits on generality remaining would be in the use of stills and the sampling of behavior from only one eliciting circumstance, posing.)

It is a tribute to the robustness of the phenomena that, despite the span of time over which this research was done and the very different theoretical

TABLE 2

Emotion Categories Proposed by Five Investigators

Woodworth 1938	Plutchik 1962	Tomkins & McCarter 1964	Osgood* 1966	Frijda** 1968b	Proposed
Love Mirth Happiness	Coyness Happiness Joy	Enjoyment Joy	Complacency Quiet pleasure Joy Glee Worried laughter	Happy	Happiness
Surprise	Surprise Amazement Astonishment	Surprise Startle	Surprise Amazement Bewilderment Awe	Surprise	Surprise
Fear	Apprehension Fear Terror	Fear Terror	Fear Horror	Fear	Fear
Suffering	Pensiveness Sorrow Grief	Distress Anguish	Despair Boredom Dreamy sadness Acute sorrow Despair	Sad	Sadness
Anger Determination	Annoyance Anger Rage	Anger Rage	Sullen Anger Rage Stubbornness Determination	Anger	Anger

TABLE 2 *cont.*

Disgust ——————— Contempt	Tiresomeness Disgust Loathing	Disgust Contempt	Annoyance Disgust Contempt Scorn Loathing	Disgust	Disgust/ Contempt
	Attentiveness Expectancy Anticipation	Interest Excitement	Expectancy Interest	Attention	Interest
	Acceptance Incorporation	Shame Humiliation	Pity Distrust Anxiety	Calm ——— Bitter ——— Pride ——— Irony ——— Insecure ——— Skepticism	

* All categories which were found in at least two of Osgood's three types of data analyses have been listed.

** All categories which emerged in the analysis of judgments of both stimulus persons have been listed.

viewpoints of the investigators, the results are by and large consistent. Table 2 shows these similarities in the categories of emotion words used to describe emotions seen in the face. All investigators proposed a *happiness* category (the only variation being Osgood's two categories for happiness), all proposed a *surprise* category, and all proposed an *anger* category. There is further agreement among all other investigators, with the exception of Woodworth. They found an *interest* category. They also combined *disgust* and *contempt* into one category. Current work by Izard (1971) and unpublished studies by Ekman and Friesen suggest that disgust and contempt may indeed be separable, as Woodworth proposed, but the evidence is still inconclusive.

The only major disagreement is that Woodworth combined "fear" and "suffering" into one category, while all the other authors kept fear as a separate category, proposing another category for words similar to *sadness*. Ekman and Friesen (1967) hypothesized that Woodworth's decision to combine the two categories was due to a failure to distinguish sadness from pain (a state not considered to be an emotion but which is associated with a discriminable facial appearance). Woodworth's term "suffering" may have been applied by observers to faces which showed either sadness or pain or the blend of both sadness and pain. There is a parallel ambiguity in the referent of Tomkins' term "anguish." It might be applicable to pain, or to the blend of sadness and pain. Boucher (1969) provided support for Ekman and Friesen's view in an experiment where stimuli which had been judged as *fear and suffering* in Woodworth's data, and stimuli which had been judged as *distress and anguish* in Tomkins and McCarter's data, were found to be judged either as *fear, sadness* or *pain*, or as blends of two of those terms, when observers were allowed only these choices. On the basis of these data, we propose that *fear* be considered a separate category, and that there should also be a separate category for *sadness*.

Table 2 also shows a number of categories which have been found or proposed by only one investigator. For the most part these categories had no opportunity to emerge from the findings of the other investigators, since these categories were not used as stimuli or judgment response by most of the other authors. Until research is done with a wide sampling of words, preferably with free choice allowed the observer, and a wide sampling of stimulus persons and emotions, it is not possible to know what to make of these other possible categories. Another unsettled question concerns the boundaries and inclusion rules for defining each category. What are the related words which might be included in a category—those which are synonyms, or those which show variations in intensity, or those which define the limits of a category? Plutchik made a beginning on this question, but there has been insufficient study.

All investigators have been interested in the related question of relationships between categories, and all but Tomkins and Frijda proposed their own set of such relationships. In addition, a number of investigators have examined their own data, searching for category relationships (e.g., Boucher & Ekman, 1965; Dickey & Knower, 1941; Dusenbury & Knower, 1938; Frois-Wittmann, 1930; Thompson & Meltzer, 1964). The data examined in most studies were consistent judgment errors, or what Tomkins and McCarter (1964) have called "common confusions." These are instances in which a stimulus judged by a majority of observers as one emotion is judged by a minority of observers as another emotion. Only two category relationships found by more than one investigator were not directly contradicted by more than one other investigator.

Fear, surprise, and interest seem to be interrelated in that fear and surprise are confused with each other, and surprise is mistaken for interest (but interest is not mistaken for surprise). Anger and disgust/contempt have also been found to be commonly confused. It should be noted that the other category relationships found by Schlosberg[7] and widely cited in textbooks have repeatedly been contradicted by other investigators, in one case in a study (Boucher and Ekman, 1965) which utilized Schlosberg's own stimuli.

It is not surprising that findings on category interrelationships have been for the most part contradictory, for the evidence used to establish common confusions is itself confusing, and most authors have been vague about their theoretical basis for expecting relationships between categories. Because of limits in the usual judgment task, common confusions might occur for two very different reasons, with quite different implications. And the term itself is probably a misnomer. One of the phenomena referred to is not a confusion at all but signifies the probable presence of a blend, while the other phenomenon is an uncommon confusion made by only a small and, in some way, unusual group of observers.

If the distribution of responses to a particular face was 60% anger and 40% disgust, the stimulus may well be a blend, containing facial components of both of these emotions (Chapter V). The confusion may be neither in the face nor with the observers, but in the fact that the investigator gave the observers only a single-response judgment task for a multiple-message stimulus. Some observers reported one response, some the other.

Work in progress (Kiritz & Ekman, 1971), entailing a judgment task which allowed observers to indicate a blend or a single emotion, found that stimuli which in previous studies, entailing a single-choice judgment task, had about a 60–40 distribution of judgment responses were now judged by the majority of the observers as showing both emotions (a blend). The use of such a judgment task, which allows the observer to record an impression of affect blends, should eliminate this type of confusion.

If the distribution of responses to a particular face was more skewed, however, let us say 80% anger and only 20% disgust, then a different phenomenon may have occurred. Kiritz and Ekman found that faces which in previous research had a distribution such as this were *not* perceived by most observers as a blend. Instead, there was a deviant minority of the observers who consistently labeled most stimuli for a particular emotion differently than the majority. In this case, they judged as disgust most of the faces which the majority called anger. The phrase "uncommon shared confusions" might describe this phenomenon. Only Tomkins and McCarter (1964) have attempted any hypotheses to explain this, and they regarded their hypotheses as only

---

[7] Schlosberg (1941) agreed with Woodworth that his six categories placed adjacent to each other formed a scale, with the exception that the two end points of the scale, *happiness* and *contempt*, should be considered as also adjacent, thus changing the linear scale into a circle; see Table 2 for the adjacent Woodworth categories.

a beginning attempt to disentangle the phenomenon. Work in progress (Zlatchin & Ekman, 1971) is investigating whether such uncommon shared confusions are related to semantic and/or personality differences.

SUMMARY

What emotion categories can observers judge from facial behavior? The question cannot yet be answered in this general form, since only still photographs and only posed behavior have been studied. However, it is possible to answer the question of what emotion categories can be judged from still photographs of posed facial behavior. Seven categories of emotion have been found (*see* the column labeled *Proposed* in Table 2): happiness, surprise, fear, anger, sadness, disgust/contempt, and interest. This is not necessarily the exhaustive list, even for posed behavior, but it appears to be the minimal list. More categories may be found in experiments which allow observers free choice of response but show them facial behavior in motion from spontaneous situations.

Such research would be particularly valuable in determining whether commonly occurring affect blends (which should be more frequent in spontaneous than posed behavior, and in motion than still presentations) will be described by the observer by combinations of these seven categories. If the choice of two or more of these categories is sufficient to permit observers to record their impressions of a stimulus containing an affect blend, then the categories can be considered primary, and the blends secondary. For example, it may be that the term "smugness" would be used to describe specific facial behavior when observers are given a free choice to use any word in their vocabulary, and that this same facial behavior would be described as both *angry* and *happy* when observers are limited to choosing among the seven categories but allowed multiple choices. If that were the result, then smugness would be considered a secondary affect blend term for the combination of anger and happiness. But if the face freely described as smug did not elicit agreement among observers in the use of two or more of the seven categories, this would suggest that there is still another primary affect category missing from that list, or that smugness itself should be included in the list of primary emotion categories.

It should be emphasized that the consistent emergence of the seven categories across the array of experiments is remarkable. Even though the studies shared the use of still posed photographs, they varied enormously in the theoretical bias of the investigators, the stimuli shown, and the judgment task employed. These seven categories of emotion seem likely to remain as a minimum group of distinctions which can be made by observers in describing facial behavior. Later (Chapter XIX) we will see further support for the generality of these categories in the findings that observers across literate and preliterate cultures agree in their use of these categories to describe facial behavior. In subsequent chapters, when we consider questions about accuracy, components of facial behavior in relation to judgments, the influence of context in the judgment of facial behavior, and cross-cultural comparisons of facial behavior, we shall employ these seven categories as the means for recasting and reanalyzing data to facilitate comparisons across experiments.

While these seven categories seem well established, there is little information about the category boundaries and interrelationships. What is the range of words which might be included within each category as synonyms, or as variants in intensity? The relationships between categories, and the possible areas of overlapping meaning, either in the terminology or facial behavior itself, have not been elucidated to date.

In the next chapter, we shall examine a different approach to the question of measuring what observers say about facial behavior, searching for *dimensions* of emotion rather than *categories*.

CHAPTER XIV

What Emotion Dimensions Can Observers Judge from Facial Behavior ?

Investigations of the dimensions of emotion, like the investigations of categories of emotion, are focused on establishing the vocabulary which can be utilized by observers of facial behavior. The theoretical model of emotion assumed by the dimensions approach is, however, quite different. Rather than considering an emotion as having a separate distinguishable status, the dimension theorists believe that an emotion could be better described and represented as a point located on a small set of continuous scales or dimensions. That is to say, rather than ask whether a facial behavior shows anger or fear or sadness, etc., these theorists have sought to determine where a facial behavior might be located along such scales as *pleasant to unpleasant, passive to active*, etc. It was important for the dimension theorists to establish the smallest number of nonredundant dimensions which would capture the information about emotion observable in the face.

There has been continuous interest in this question from the 1940's to the present time, in contrast to the disjunctive history of research activity on many of the other questions we will consider. Schlosberg (1941) was the first investigator to attempt to derive a minimal set of scales for the judgment of emotion from facial behavior, proposing first a two- and then a three-dimensional model (1954) which he thought might underlie Woodworth's six categories of emotion. His interest in dimensions, and that of subsequent investigators, stemmed from two sources. Obtaining ordinal or interval data by the use of scales rather than nominal data from the use of emotion categories offered statistical techniques for obtaining better measures of agreement among observers. And, the discovery of a set of scales which could best account for judgments of emotion from the face might be relevant to a more general theory of emotion. Osgood (1966) recently reiterated this view, suggesting that scales can produce better agreement than categories, not merely because of the advantage of continuous scaled data over nominal data, but because scales which represent connotative meaning (e.g., the three factors from his semantic differential work in verbal behavior) are more relevant to the kind of information provided by the face than are any denotative emotion categories.

Two types of experiments have been conducted. In one, observers judged faces on a set of scales provided by the investigator; in the other, observers rated the amount of similarity between pairs of faces, usually without the investigator or the observer specifying the basis for judgment or type of similarity being judged. In both types of experiment the sampling of stimulus persons, emotions, and eliciting circumstances is crucial. Almost all of the experiments can be faulted on several grounds, but there are additional methodological problems particular to each of the two types of experiments.

Table 3 lists the methodological decisions crucial to the studies in which the observers judged faces on a set of scales or terms. As in the studies of emotion categories discussed earlier, posing has been the sole eliciting circumstance employed. Just as serious a problem is the use of a very few stimulus persons,[8] because the dimension results could have reflected their idiosyncracies.[9] The number of stimuli shown appears adequate in most studies, as does the number of emotions represented in those stimuli. (The latter is not known for the Hastorf, Osgood, & Ono study, nor for the Frijda & Philipszoon experiment; Fridja has acknowledged Stringer's (1967) evidence that anger was underrepresented in their study.) In most of the studies from 6 to 13 categories were represented, the stimuli having been judged also in terms of emotion categories, the results of which were reported in Table 2.

There is serious question about the number of scales or terms provided the judges in two of these studies, and about the basis of selecting those scales. Schlosberg (1952, 1954) and Hastorf, Osgood, and Ono (1966) provided the smallest number of scales for judgment, and used only the scales they

---

[8] While Osgood's sample of 50 persons is larger than any of the other samples, the fact that only five persons posed each emotion allows a small number of persons to bias the results; *see* page 58.

[9] Frijda's factor analysis of judgments of three separate stimulus persons (his two actors and the actor in Schlosberg's Lightfoot pictures), was reassuring, in that the same factors emerged for all three; the problems remain, however, that all three were actors, all were posing emotions specifically for a psychological study of emotion dimensions, and a sample of three is very small.

TABLE 3

Methodological Considerations for Studies of Emotion Dimensions

	Schlosberg 1954	Osgood 1966	Hastorf Osgood Ono 1966	Frijda Philipszoon 1963	Frijda** 1968a	Frijda 1968b
1. Number of Different Stimulus Persons	3	50 or 5*	1	1	1	2
2. Number of Different Emotions Represented in Stimuli	6	40 intents 9 categories from judgment results		Not Reported	Not Reported	13 categories from judgment results
3. Number of Stimuli	200	200	35	30	Not Reported	130
4. Number of Scales or Terms Given the Observers	3	40 labels	12	22	28	40
5. Method of Deriving the Scales or Terms	inspection of photographs	past literature	chosen because of high factor loadings on Osgood's 3 dimensions	most frequent in free naming	Not Reported	Not Reported
6. Eliciting Circumstance	pose	pose	pose	pose	pose	pose
7. Recording Technique	stills	live	stills	stills	stills	stills
8. Evidence for Authors' Model	scale scores predict category judgments	factor analysis	factor analysis	factor analysis	factor analysis	factor analysis

* See discussion on page 58.

** This study used the Schlosberg Lightfoot stimuli.

69

thought relevant to their theory. Needless to say, both confirmed their expectation that there are but three dimensions of emotion, while in the studies using more scales, more factors were found (*see* Table 4).

Another serious problem germane to almost all of the experiments is ambiguity about what aspect of the face and emotion the investigator is attempting to study or represent in his dimensions, and the inclusion in his scales of words which refer to quite different aspects of the phenomenon. Are the judges asked to evaluate the physical appearance of the face?[10] The subjective feelings of the person?[11] The genuineness of the poses?[12] Connotations of words in general?[13] Defenses or ways of coping with emotion, or action consequences?[14] The more enduring personality traits or attitudes, rather than transient emotions?[15] There is no argument with attempting to determine whether observers can agree about each of these aspects of emotion; it would be interesting to compare dimensions which emerged from a factor analysis in which sets of scales for each of these aspects of emotion were systematically represented. The problem is that some investigators have utilized scales which differ among themselves in the aspects of emotion referred to, without explicitly acknowledging that or examining their data in light of that fact. Others have utilized terms for one aspect of emotion in their scales, and then argued for the generality of their dimensions without acknowledging that other dimensions might well have emerged if scales relevant to other aspects of emotion had been included.

A last inadequacy of most of these studies is in the use of still photographs rather than videotape or motion picture film recordings of facial behavior.[16]

As was noted in discussing the results across a number of experiments on categories, while the findings from any single experiment are open to serious question because of major methodological defects, by summarizing the common findings across a number of experiments, at least those methodological shortcomings which have limited the generality of the findings become

---

[10] E.g., Schlosberg's attention-rejection scale was defined for his observers as, "the person is making every effort to see something, or the person is trying to shut out or keep out stimulation."

[11] E.g., Schlosberg's, Frijda's, and Osgood's pleasant-unpleasant scale, or Frijda's happy-sad scale.

[12] E.g., Frijda's artificial-natural scale.

[13] E.g., Osgood's and Frijda's soft-hard, or deep-shallow scales.

[14] E.g., Osgood's and Frijda's controlled-uncontrolled scale, and Frijda's withdrawing-approaching scale.

[15] E.g., Frijda's authoritarian-submissive scale.

[16] While Osgood used live performance, problems with that procedure were earlier outlined (*see* page 50).

TABLE 4

Dimensions Found by the Investigators Who Had Observers Judge Faces Using Scales or Terms

	Schlosberg 1954	Osgood 1966	Hastorf Osgood Ono 1966	Frijda Philip-szoon* 1963	Frijda** 1968a	Frijda 1968b
Pleasant-Unpleasant	×	×	×	×	×	×
Attention-Rejection	×					
Sleep-Tension	×					
Activation		×	×			
Control (Osgood) Emotional Intensity-Control (Frijda)		×	×	×	×	×
Interest (Osgood) Attentional Activity (Frijda)		×		×	×	×
Social Evaluation or Natural-Artificial				×	×	×
Surprise				×		×
Simple-Complicated				×		×
Strength					×	
Positive-Negative Social Attitude					×	
Self-Assertive—Dependence						×

* Frijda's reanalysis in 1969 of this data is reported.
** This study used Schlosberg's Lightfoot photographs as stimuli.

less crucial. In considering this set of experiments on dimensions, the need for broad sampling of persons and of emotions is at least partly met by considering the results across all the experiments listed in Tables 3 and 4. However, problems remain, both in regard to determining the limits on generality because only posed still photographs were studied and, perhaps most importantly, in regard to explaining the lack of consistent findings across studies, because the number, sampling, and method of deriving scales have varied widely. Table 4 shows that the only consistent finding across experiments is a dimension of Pleasantness/Unpleasantness. If we are willing to consider Osgood's interest factor as similar to Frijda's Attentional Activity (which is how Frijda interpreted Osgood's factor), and also to consider Schlosberg's Attention-Rejection as similar to Frijda's Attentional Activity (and Frijda reported a high factor loading of that bipolar scale with this factor), then there would be a second common finding in all but one study— Attentional Activity. Again if we consider Osgood's control factor to be comparable to Frijda's Emotional Intensity-Control, which is how Frijda interpreted his own and Osgood's result, then with the exception of Schlosberg, we have a third common finding, an Intensity-Control factor. Beyond those three factors, the findings are not very consistent even within the work of a single investigator such as Frijda, when he varied the stimulus persons judged.

The investigators listed in the table disagree about how many dimensions are necessary. Osgood and Schlosberg held that three dimensions are enough to account for the full range of emotional expression; Frijda believed there must be at least five. Applying Osgood's injunction that evidence for more dimensions from studies which sampled many scales be given greater weight than evidence for fewer dimensions from studies which sampled few scales, and applying a similar injunction in regard to representative sampling of stimulus persons, we would suggest that Frijda's and Osgood's findings be given more weight than Schlosberg's, or those of Hastorf, Osgood, and Ono. More than three dimensions are probably necessary; what these might be remains an unsettled question.

Let us turn now from the method of studying dimensions in which observers judge faces on some set of scales to the method in which observers rate similarity. Abelson and Sermat (1962) pointed out that the verbal labels chosen by the experimenter to define the observer's rating scales may impose on the observer a form of response not normally elicited by facial behavior. A number of investigators attempted to avoid this biasing effect by asking their observers to rate pairs of stimuli in terms of global similarity. Unfortunately, this judgment procedure has its own set of problems.

Most of these studies have used only one stimulus person, and very few samples of that person's behavior, probably because all possible pairs of the stimuli must be shown to the observer for judgment. If 20 or 30 stimuli were to be included, the number of paired judgments required would be very large. There has often been a lack of assurance that the few stimuli provided a representative sampling of different emotions (e.g., *see* page 73 for our analysis of how this pertains to the Abelson & Sermat experiment).

Frijda (1968a) suggested that there may be a lack of comparability between findings from similarity rating experiments and dimension rating experiments, because the two judgment tasks require different cognitive operations:

There is a distinct difference in task between labeling or scale rating on the one hand, and similarity estimation on the other, as Stringer (1967) himself pointed out. In the first, the subject is asked to discriminate aspects; in the second, to overlook differences, to search for similarities.

A major problem noted with the experiments in which judgments are made on scales is the quite various aspects of the phenomenon to which the scales might refer. A parallel in the similarity studies is the possible ambiguity about what the observer should or does attend to when judging a pair of faces. Similarities could be judged in terms of the appearance of the facial muscles, or in terms of inferred feeling states, or in terms of likely action consequences, or, if different stimulus persons are included, on the basis of physiognomic or demographic variables. If the observer is overlooking differences and searching for some basis to assess similarity, as Frijda suggested, then the observer might consider a different kind of similarity (appearance, feeling, etc.) for each pair of stimuli he judges.

In analyzing similarity judgments, some investigators have found evidence for two independent dimensions, others for three. Abelson and Sermat found two dimensions—Pleasantness and Activation—as did Shepard (1963) and Kauranne (1964). Nummenmaa and Kauranne (1958) and Nummenmaa (1964) found evidence for two dimensions, but they replaced the Activation dimension with a dimension more like Schlosberg's Attention/Rejection. Their two dimensions were described as Pleasant/Anger and Surprise/Rejection, with each varying in intensity.

Royal and Hays (1959) and Gladstones (1962) discovered evidence for three dimensions. Both discerned a Pleasantness and an Activation dimension, but they differed in their third dimension. Stringer (1967, 1968a, 1968b) also performed a similarity analysis and perceived three dimensions, and while one of them—Happy/Worry—is similar to Pleasantness, the other two are different from those proposed by anyone else (Thoughtful/Surprise and Thoughtful/Disgust/Pain).

SUMMARY

An answer cannot be given to the general question under consideration, since only still photographic records of only posed behavior have been studied, but it is possible to provide a partial answer to a more limited question. What emotion dimensions can observers judge from still photographs of posed facial behavior? In the studies based on the facial behavior of more than one person (Osgood, 1966; Frijda, 1968a) with extensive sampling of emotion words in the scales, the evidence suggested at least four or five dimensions. Certainly, one of these dimensions is something like Pleasantness/ Unpleasantness, another Activation or Intensity. Beyond that, there is little consensus among authors. Part of the problem is the limited sampling of persons, stimuli and scales; part of the difficulty is that the authors had very different hypotheses about what the dimensions might be (e.g., Osgood believed the dimensions should be the same as the dimensions of semantic meaning found in his studies of verbal behavior; Frijda believed the dimensions should refer to action tendencies).

Schlosberg, Osgood, and Frijda all proposed that their dimensions were related to the emotion categories. But Schlosberg and Osgood thought there were fixed relationships among emotion categories which would locate them within geometric models of the emotion dimensions. Frijda, on the other hand, proposed a hierarchical model, which allowed the emotion categories to be independent of each other, though sharing on another level of consideration attributes or qualities which were represented by the dimensions. This question of the relationship between judgment of emotion categories and judgment of emotion dimensions is far from settled.

It seems doubtful that consistent findings about dimensions of emotion will be found until investigators utilize stimuli which have been shown by other means to represent a number of different emotion categories (at least those listed in Table 2), until they sample the behavior of many different persons, and until they select scales which systematically represent all or, at least, many of the aspects of emotion which might be judged from the face— appearance, feeling, action consequences, etc. It would be useful to compare findings from both scale judgment and similarity judgment experiments in which the same set of faces have been judged and the same referents represented in the scale terms and in instructions about the aspects of similarity which should be judged.

Some of the dimension theorists (e.g., Frijda) believe that the judgment task they employ, rating a face on a series of scales, is much closer to the phenomenology of how people actually do perceive faces in nonexperimental settings, than is the judgment task employed in the emotion category approach in which the observer is asked to choose among such categories as fear, anger, sadness, etc. Their thinking seems to be that in usual social intercourse either the face doesn't provide enough information for us to make the category distinction, or we just do not respond to and think about faces in that way. Of course, some of the emotion category theorists (e.g., Tomkins) hold just the opposite view, that in actual social intercourse people respond to other people's facial behavior in terms just like those used in the categories approach: he is angry, afraid, sad, etc.

There are no data available on this question. We do not know the vocabulary utilized by observers who witness social interaction, hearing as well as seeing, knowing the social context, and observing the sequence of behavior which occurs. Nor do we know the thoughts and vocabulary of the interactants themselves at those points at which they may attend to or comment on each other's facial behavior. Though it would be important to determine which approach—categories or dimensions—is more similar to the phenomenology of social interaction, this is not the sole or even necessarily the most important criterion for choosing between these two schemes and judgment tasks.

One may also ask, which approach offers the more economical approach for measuring emotional information? That is, which employs the smallest number of independent variables to account for the information observed from the face? Probably the dimensions approach does, but the matter is not settled. Which approach allows more sophisticated statistical treatment in data analysis? Certainly the use of continuous scales is preferable to data from nominal categories. Which approach allows finer discriminations by observers? The data are not definitive on this question, although it may be that the category approach may allow more distinctions. Evidence on this matter could be derived from studies in which observers' judgments are linked to measurements of facial components (*see* Chapter XVII). Although one study has successfully linked facial components to observers' judgments on emotion categories, the dimension approach has not received a sufficient test, since the one experiment on this question where observers had judged faces utilizing dimensions did not employ an adequate measure of facial components.

It is not possible, then, from the evidence reviewed in this and the preceding chapter, to say whether a categories or dimensions approach is preferable. The investigator will have to choose according to his hunch, his theoretical bias or, perhaps, his preferred method of data analysis. If he selects a category approach, we have proposed that he include at least the seven categories of emotion which have been consistently found in past research. If he selects a dimension approach, he should include scales relevant to pleasantness/unpleasantness, attentional activity, and intensity/control. Beyond these three, he should take note of the evidence which suggests that probably two or three more dimensions are necessary, but it is not clear what they are.

CHAPTER XV

Can Judgments of Emotion
from Facial Behavior Be Accurate?

The question of whether the face can provide accurate[17] information about emotion has been the central issue since the beginning of research on the face. Even though there might well be legitimate research questions if the face provides only inaccurate information, for example, in understanding a source of stereotyping and misinformation in person perception, the determination of accuracy has been pivotal in the ebb and flow of research activity on the face. In this chapter we shall document our claim that there is now sufficient evidence of accurate information to merit renewed and vigorous research on the face and emotion. In so doing, we shall directly challenge the misinterpretations, based in part on misinformation, provided by past reviewers of this work.

Although either a judgment or a component approach (*see* Chapter VI) could be employed in experiments on accuracy, almost all of the research has used a judgment design. We will consider the few studies which examined accuracy by measuring facial components in the next chapter.

The question of whether *observers* could make accurate judgments of emotion was the key issue in the first period of research from 1914 to 1940, and the answer to this question was an important determinant of interest in the

---

[17] The reader may wish to refer to Chapter II where the problems of establishing accuracy criteria were discussed. Accuracy was defined as correct information of some nature being obtained by some means from facial behavior. As such, accuracy does not necessarily entail accurate information about emotion; relevance of the accuracy to some aspect of the phenomena described as emotional must be demonstrated, in addition to the finding of accuracy. Major methodological problems encountered in the main types of accuracy criteria which will be discussed in the present section were reviewed. In this chapter, we will say that an author obtained evidence of accuracy whenever the observers were correct more often than would be expected by chance ($p < 0.05$).

face and emotion, with the exception of those who turned to the study of the vocabulary of emotion judgments. In their highly influential reviews of this literature, Bruner and Tagiuri (1954) and Tagiuri (1968) wrote:

> Some writers have reported that, whatever the nature of the expressive stimulus, the number of correct recognitions of emotions on the part of their subjects did not exceed the number that would be expected on a chance basis (for example, Fernberger, 1927, 1928; Guilford, 1929; Jarden & Fernberger, 1926; Landis, 1924, 1929; Sherman, 1927a—all of whom employed photographs of real emotions elicited in the laboratory). Others have shown that emotional expressions can be labeled with considerable accuracy (for example, Darwin, 1872; Feleky, 1914; Goodenough, 1931; Langfeld, 1918; Levitt, 1964; Levy, 1964; Munn, 1940; Ruckmick, 1921; Schulze, 1912; Stratton, 1921; Thompson and Meltzer, 1964; Woodworth, 1938) (1954, p. 635; 1968, p. 399).

It is no wonder that investigators might lose interest in this uninviting topic, or at the least in the question of whether the face provides valid information about emotion. But Bruner and Tagiuri were factually incorrect and misleading. They enhanced the credibility of the negative findings on accuracy by saying that all of those experimenters utilized photographs of real emotions elicited in the laboratory. This is true only of Landis and Sherman. Fernberger, Guilford, and Jarden and Fernberger, whom they also credited with such laudable research methods, instead studied artists' drawings, not photographs, of posed or remembered behavior, not of real emotions elicited in the laboratory. Guilford studied the Rudolf faces, which are sketches made from photographs of an actor posing; Fernberger, and Jarden and Fernberger studied the Boring and Titchener (1923) version of Piderit's drawings of the face, which *presumed* to show emotions in terms of separate facial features.[18] The negative studies which remain in Bruner and Tagiuri's list, those of Landis and of Sherman, had been widely criticized and at least partially contradicted in the literature prior to their 1954 review.

No research on accuracy has been performed which completely satisfies the requirements outlined earlier in our methodological framework. Nevertheless, we will show that for studies of posed behavior reliable evidence of accurate judgment can be obtained by taking into account findings across a number of experiments; judgments do coincide with the posers' intent.

---

[18] Earlier (pages 50–51), we discussed the reasons why the use of drawings of the face have only the most dubious relevance to studies of accuracy, and why we have excluded all such studies from this review. Among the studies Bruner and Tagiuri cited as providing positive evidence on accuracy, we have excluded Langfeld because he also used the Rudolf faces, Levy and Stratton because they did not study the face, Schulze because his book was not available, and Ruckmick because there were only nine observers.

Although there is not as much evidence in regard to spontaneous behavior, what there is suggests a positive rather than a negative answer. Before considering these studies, however, we will first analyze the Landis and the Sherman experiments, bringing together past criticisms, our own framework, and relevant other experiments which raise doubts about their findings, in an attempt finally to lay these two experiments to rest.

A. THE LANDIS AND COLEMAN EXPERIMENTS

Landis took still photographs of his 25 subjects in a series of 17 situations, which included listening to music, looking at pornographic pictures, smelling ammonia, being shocked, decapitating a live rat, etc. Brief introspective reports were obtained after each situation, but these were kept short because Landis wanted a "cumulative disturbance" (an aim which provides the basis for one of the methodological criticisms to be discussed shortly). Four of the subjects were later asked to remember each situation and pose a facial behavior for each. Photographs were taken by the investigator when he noticed a change in the face. Landis selected 77 from the 844 photographs for use in his judgment study; 56 were from the initial situations, 21 from the remembered, posed situations; the sampling included the behavior of 22 stimulus persons. Landis said he selected pictures for use in his judgment study which he thought were expressive. Forty-two observers judged the photographs, describing in their own words the emotion felt by the stimulus person, the situation which might have elicited the reaction, and their feeling of certainty about their judgment.

Landis reported that the results clearly showed that the emotions judged and the situations described by the observers were completely irrelevant to both the actual and the posed situations, and to the introspective reports made during the actual situations. He attributed the discrepancy between the inaccuracy of his observers and the accuracy found by other investigators to the latter having used posed facial behavior, considered by Landis to be a specialized, conventional, language-like behavior which does not occur when people actually feel emotion.

While there are many grounds for criticizing Landis' experiment, we will look into only three of these which can, at least in part, be supported by re-examination of Landis' data.

Davis (1934) in his reanalysis of Landis' data on the components of facial behavior (a separate study by Landis of the records from this experiment), found a tendency for the behaviors shown in the later situations to correlate with each other more than with the earlier situations. Davis interpreted this as due to the cumulative effect of experiencing the various situations in Landis' experiment and, as noted above, Landis purposefully kept the subjects' self-reports brief in order to enhance a cumulative disturbance. But, if the disturbance was cumulative, if there was a tendency for the emotions experienced in one situation to carry over to the next, and for a disturbed or stressed reaction to build up, it would have been extremely difficult for observers when they saw the facial behavior from each situation either to discriminate separate, different emotions or to guess the specific eliciting circumstance. Only if the situations are not cumulative, only if each situation elicits a different reaction, would there be a chance for differing facial responses to occur which could provide a systematic basis for the observer to appraise the particular emotion or situation when viewing a particular face. (Coleman, 1949, took Davis' criticism of Landis' experiment seriously, built rest periods into his experiment to diminish any cumulative effect, and attributed his positive results to his succeeding in eliminating a cumulative effect. We will consider Coleman's study shortly.)

A second criticism of Landis' experiment, first raised by Frois-Wittmann (1930), is that Landis' situations may not have elicited the same emotion in all of his subjects; Arnold (1960) and Honkavaara (1961) later raised the same question. Further, it is possible that each situation might have evoked more than one emotion, either simultaneously as a blend, or consecutively. Looking at pornographic pictures, for example, or reading Kraft-Ebbing case histories, might elicit disgust in one subject, happiness in another, disgust-anger in a third, etc. If such variations did occur, then it would be highly unlikely that observers would be able to achieve accuracy on one of Landis' two accuracy criteria, correctly guessing the eliciting circumstance. But his other accuracy criterion, the subject's self-report of his experience, could provide a more useful basis for measuring accuracy since, if subjects responded differently and reported those differences, observers might correctly judge information related to those self-reports, even if they failed to identify the eliciting circumstance.

Such was not the case; Landis explained failure on this accuracy criterion as due to error inherent in such flimsy data as introspection. After considering the criticism under review, that Landis' situations were not emotion-specific across subjects, we will consider a third criticism, that Landis' experimental procedures led his subjects to mask or control their facial behavior and not to reveal their actual feelings. If that were so, then self-report would indeed be a poor source of information for establishing accuracy.

Let us examine now two aspects of Landis' data which support this second criticism, that the eliciting situations were not emotion-specific across subjects. Landis' listing of the subjects' introspective reports shows that only in two of his 17 situations did even half of his stimulus persons report feeling the same emotion. Furthermore, his observers failed to judge accurately the posed facial behavior which his subjects recreated for these situations, thus contradicting Landis' belief that stereotyped posed behaviors *would be* accurately judged. Landis did not attempt to explain why his observers were unable to judge his subjects' poses accurately. An explanation consistent with the second criticism is that most of his 17 situations were probably not associated with any single emotion for all of his posers, who thus emitted various facial behaviors depending on the emotion they believed to be associated with a given situation. Landis' negative results on the judgment of spontaneous behavior in his situations would be more credible if he had found that poses of behavior thought to be relevant to these situations could be accurately judged.

The third basis for criticism, first made by Murphy, Murphy, and Newcomb (1937), and repeated by Arnold and by Honkavaara, is that Landis may have unintentionally encouraged his subjects to inhibit or mask their facial responses to his situations. Landis mentioned this possibility but, unaccountably, dismissed it. A number of aspects of the experimental setting indicate the operation of display rules either to neutralize the facial responses or to mask them with a positive affect. All of Landis' subjects knew him; most were psychologists who had had other laboratory experiences. Not only did they know they were being photographed, but, because Landis had marked their faces with burnt cork in order to measure the components of facial behavior in his other use of these records, they knew Landis was interested in their facial behavior.[19]

Some aspects of Landis' results are consistent with this criticism. Landis reported that smiles were frequent in all of his situations, though he was convinced that his subjects were not feeling happy. Landis interpreted this as evidence against the meaningfulness of the smile; we would interpret it as possible evidence of masking. A second source of support for the contention that Landis' experiment encouraged the operation of masking and neutralizing display rules is the introspective data. More than a third of the 17 situations elicited a report of "no feeling" from the majority of the subjects. If that is true, Landis failed with some frequency to elicit emotion. However,

---

[19] It is interesting to note that Hunt (1941), a supporter of Landis, belittled the importance of Munn's (1940) accuracy findings on the grounds that his subjects might have known they were being photographed, but failed to consider that this criticism was even more applicable to Landis.

these self-reports, which he did not believe, do appear improbable in view of the anecdotal evidence he provided and the experience of others with such eliciting circumstances. The alternative, then, is that the reports of no feeling suggest an unwillingness to acknowledge being emotionally aroused, which could well have been duplicated in the facial behavior. In a completely different situation, Ekman and Friesen (1969a) have provided some evidence that when an individual wants to conceal his feelings and mask his emotions with a socially acceptable feeling, the face typically either displays the deceptive mask or conveys contradictory information. This may well have happened in Landis' experiment.

In sum, Landis' findings that observers could not make accurate judgments, either as compared to the expected emotional nature of the eliciting circumstance or the subject's self-reported experience, should be credited only if (a) the same or similar reactions were elicited during at least some of the situations in most of the subjects, (b) the elicited reactions were different for at least some of the different situations, and (c) the selection of subjects and experimental arrangements did not encourage the subjects to mask or otherwise to control their facial behavior and/or to falsify their self-report.[20] The three criticisms discussed suggest that these conditions were probably not met.

The last argument against Landis' findings is based on Coleman's (1949) study with comparable eliciting circumstances, in which the observers *did* achieve accuracy. Coleman took motion picture film of the facial responses of six men and six women to eight situations comparable to Landis' and of their subsequent attempts to pose the appropriate facial response for each situation. Because Coleman's interest was in comparing judgments of the top and bottom half of the face, which required the tedious chore of blacking out part of each motion picture frame, he utilized the films of only two of the 12 persons in his judgment experiment. He said he selected stimulus persons whose behavior he believed to be natural, not exaggerated, but showing a variety of expressions, and whose self-reports revealed that they were strongly affected by the experiment. Later we will consider his results on the judgments of the partial faces, and consider now only his results on the judgments of the full faces.

The motion picture films of the natural or original responses and the posed responses of two subjects were shown to 379 observers, who judged

---

[20] Our analysis does not presume that all of these problems operated in a similar fashion for all subjects. Some may have shown the cumulative disturbance, others may have been more concerned with concealing their responses; it is also possible that concealment was more salient at the beginning of the experiment for most subjects, while toward the end the effects of the cumulative disturbance became manifest.

which of nine situations was the one the film clip had been taken in; in addition to the eight actual situations, a ninth was added to decrease judgment by elimination. Judgments were accurate, in that the correct situations were identified for each stimulus person, in both the natural and posed versions, more than would be expected by chance. Posing enhanced accuracy, but for different situations for the two stimulus persons.

Why did Coleman obtain positive and Landis negative results?

1. Coleman's situations might have elicited more similar emotions across his two stimulus persons, with different reactions to at least some of the situations by both subjects. Coleman did, after all, purposefully select subjects whom he thought had been affected by the experiment, which might mean that he picked those who had shown or reported different experiences across his eight situations. Coleman explained the difference in his results from Landis' as due to his inclusion of rest periods to diminish any cumulative disturbance which might obscure different reactions to his eight situations. Evidence in support of the possibility that most of Coleman's situations were associated with different emotions, and by both subjects, comes from his positive results on the judgment of posed behavior. Landis' failure to obtain accuracy in judgments of posed behavior suggests, it will be recalled, that his subjects may not have shared the same emotional experience and therefore did not attempt to pose the same emotions. The fact that Coleman did obtain accuracy in judgments of posed behavior suggests, contrarily, that at least some of his situations were associated with the same emotion by his two subjects.

2. Coleman's judgment task may have allowed for more complex or inferential judgments in that he did not ask his observers to judge emotion, as did Landis, but instead to pick the situation during which a film was taken. If an observer sees a subject smile, and knows nothing of the situation, he may simply call that smile "happy." But if he knows the nature of the various eliciting situations, he may well consider the possibility that the smile is a mask, or an embarrassed reaction to the feelings elicited by one of the situations (e.g., Coleman's situation of crushing a snail). Coleman's judgment task of matching a situation with a film clip leaves open, however, the question of whether the accuracy obtained was dependent upon information about emotion. Perhaps accurate judgments could have been based upon behavior not usually described as emotional; i.e., defensive behavior. It would be helpful if Coleman had shown the same films to another group of observers and asked them to judge the emotions shown.

3. Coleman showed motion picture films, while Landis obtained judgments on still photographs. Earlier, we argued that films or videotape were more

appropriate than stills for recording spontaneous behavior since they would not fragment the natural flow of behavior. Still photographs are more appropriate to record static poses. While Landis fired his camera whenever he thought something was happening, his basic unit, a single still, would provide less information about the onset and duration of the facial response, even if his own reaction time was so rapid that he adequately captured the response at its apex or most extreme moment. The type of complex, inferential judgment referred to above would probably be easier to make from films, which show the sequence of reactions, duration, etc., than from still photographs.

4. Coleman's subjects might have been less motivated to inhibit or mask their facial behavior than Landis' subjects. Unlike Landis, Coleman did not select subjects who knew him, nor did he mark their faces; thus he may have avoided Landis' error of inadvertently encouraging the operation of those display rules which inhibit candid facial responses.

Certainly Coleman's study is far from conclusive as an accuracy study. The generality of the findings across persons cannot be determined with only two stimulus persons nor, for reasons just mentioned, can it be determined that the accuracy obtained necessarily involved judgments of emotion. But Coleman's study does underline the three major methodological problems in Landis' experiment, and strengthens our contention that the results of Landis' experiment should be discredited. Correcting some of the flaws in Landis' experiment, Coleman was able to achieve accuracy. It is regrettable that no further work has been done utilizing such eliciting circumstances, for the most conclusive evidence for discounting Landis' findings would be further studies similar to Coleman's with a larger number of stimulus persons.

B. THE SHERMAN EXPERIMENT

The only other study which obtained negative results on accuracy among those described by Bruner and Tagiuri (1954) and Tagiuri (1968) as utilizing real behavior elicited in the laboratory, and which actually did so, was Sherman's (1927a) study of observers' judgments of very young infants. His research has remained influential despite challenges to his interpretation of his results as long ago as 1931 by Goodenough, again by Murphy, Murphy, and Newcomb (1937), and recently by Honkavaara (1961), and despite the results of other inquiries which contradicted his findings. As with Landis, we will critically examine his results in detail, not because of the merits of his study, but because of its continuing acceptance despite enormous flaws. We will suggest a number of grounds for challenging the validity of his results, as well as his interpretation of them, and will present a summary of contradictory results from a number of studies from the same era.

Sherman actually performed four separate experiments, with different conditions, only one of which is sufficiently free of confounding sources of variability to be considered. In that experiment, he recorded on motion picture film the behavior of two infants, one 74 hours old and the other 145 hours old, as they were subjected to four eliciting circumstances: hunger, defined as missing the infants' scheduled feeding by 15 minutes;[21] suddenly dropping the infant; restraining the infant by holding the head and face down on a table; and applying a needle to the cheek six times. Two groups of observers (graduate and freshman psychology students) were shown the behavior immediately after the elicitation and asked to judge the emotion and the eliciting circumstance in their own words.

His second experiment was said to be the only instance in which accuracy and agreement were achieved. Here, the observers saw not only the post-elicitation films, but also the filmed behavior during the elicitation itself. The results are difficult to interpret for the following reasons. These observers had two, not one, sources of additional information: knowledge of the eliciting circumstance, which Sherman intended, and access to the full range of the infants' facial behavior during the elicitation procedure, which may have been redundant with or different from the post-elicitation facial behavior shown in the first experiment. Another problem in comparing the results from the first and second experiment is that Sherman coached the subjects in the second experiment about what behaviors to observe, but not in the first experiment. A third problem is that half of the observers in the second experiment had been observers in the first study. Any difference in performance between the first and second experiment could be due, then, not only to coaching, or knowledge of elicitor, or exposure to additional facial behavior during elicitation, but also to the benefits of practice or memory for the observers who had already been in the first experiment.

The third set of data was gathered from medical students and nurses who were shown the live, not the recorded, post-elicitation behavior of an unspecified number of infants. (A screen blocking their view was present during elicitation and then removed.) We have rejected these data because the judgments are confounded by the observers' exposure not only to the facial behavior as in the first study, but also, as Sherman readily acknowledged,

---

[21] Sherman does not explain the basis for the presumption that in infants of that young age the feeding schedule is sufficiently established for a 15-minute deviation to be a noticeable difference sufficient to elicit any reaction. It is to be hoped that Sherman had other bases for knowing that his two infants were hungry at the time of the experiment.

to the vocal behavior; all infants cried during post-elicitation. We might note, lest the reader think he is missing important material, that these two groups of observers were small, and that in most instances, the majority of their judgments were of events, not emotions, e.g., colic, just awakening, tight bandage.

The last study is one in which the eliciting circumstance film from one situation was followed by the post-elicitation film from another situation as if they were sequential. This experiment suffers from most of the same flaws as that in which the observers saw the films of the actual eliciting circumstance in addition to the post-elicitation films.

Our decision, based upon methodological flaws in all of the other experiments, to consider only the data from the first experiment, in which observers saw only the post-elicitation behavior, does not ignore the results Sherman himself considered crucial. Sherman interpreted the data from that experiment as most damaging to any claim that accurate judgments could be made from infants' facial behavior.

There are three major flaws in Sherman's first experiment which serve to raise serious doubt about the validity of his conclusion. First, Sherman's data analysis is oversimplified. He did not distinguish between judgments of emotion, utilizing the usual emotion vocabulary, and judgments of events or internal states, i.e., taking medicine or being hungry. Instead, he counted both types of responses in his measures of whether observers could make accurate emotion judgments. Further, he ignored the possibility that some of the emotion terms might have been synonyms, although F. Allport had published his emotion categories a few years earlier (1924); thus, Sherman considered rage and anger, for example, as different emotion judgments, and pain and hurt as different judgments.

The second and more serious criticism of Sherman's experiment is the probability that all four situations may well have elicited the *same* reaction from the infants and, of course, as explained earlier in connection with Landis, if the situations do not elicit different reactions, then there is little reason to expect the observer to make different judgments. In other words, Sherman's accuracy criterion was the emotion *he* expected in each of his four situations; but he provided no empirical basis for his expectation and, if he was wrong, if the situations all elicited the same response, then the failure to find accurate judgments is meaningless. Two aspects of Sherman's data suggest that the reactions across the four stimulus situations were similar. Anger was the most frequent judgment for all four of his situations, which Sherman saw as evidence of inaccuracy; but quite conceivably his infants *were* angry, either during all four situations or *after* each of the four stimulus situations. For it must be remembered that we are considering judgments made of behavior post-elicitation; it could be that the four elicitations each produced a distinctive response immediately, that was rapidly dissipated a few moments later, and would not have been seen in the post-elicitation behavior, which may well have shown anger. Honkavaara (1961) may have had this in mind in criticizing Sherman for sampling infant behavior only during crying. From Sherman's other article (1927b) describing a separate study in which observers listened to the sounds made by the infants but did not see the films (again, failing to achieve accuracy in terms of Sherman's expectations), Honkavaara discovered that the infants in the study we are here discussing cried in all four of the post-elicitation situations. While crying does not necessarily signify that *only* anger, or only some other emotion, was present in the post-elicitation behavior, one must question whether Sherman really did succeed in preserving different emotions for the four situations, without which he could have no basis for interpreting his results as showing inaccuracy.

The third criticism of Sherman's experiments, raised by Goodenough (1931), Murphy, Murphy, and Newcomb (1937), and Honkavaara (1961) has to do with the age of the infants, both less than one week old. The failure of such young infants to show a differentiated facial response across the four eliciting situations would not be a conclusive demonstration that the face is unrelated to emotion, nor that social learning provides the sole basis for any such relationship which might exist later. Maturation might be such that the differentiated perception of the situations necessary for differential facial response, or the differentiation of the facial responses themselves, might not have unfolded prior to an age of 150 hours.

The last criticism is that a sample of two infants is far too small to permit any conclusions; and, further, Sherman did not report his data separately for the judgments of the 74-hour and the 145-hour infant, so it cannot be determined whether the observers' judgments were similar for both or different because of maturational or other factors.

Although we will not consider as a separate substantive issue the nature of the development of facial behaviors associated with emotion, we will explore four articles reporting findings which indirectly contradict Sherman's to complete the case we have constructed for dismissing Sherman's experiment.

Goodenough (1931) showed eight photographs of a ten-month-old infant to 68 observers. The observers were given a choice among 12 possible judgments, each judgment describing both an emotion and an eliciting situation. There were four more choices provided than stimuli to decrease the chance that the observers would choose by elimination. Goodenough reported that 47% of the judgments were accurate. In our reanalysis of her data, we first discarded all of the stimuli and judgments which involved the description of facial appearance rather than an inference about emotion (satisfied smile; roguish smiling; crying). We also omitted two stimuli which were described too generally to be relevant to accuracy regarding specific emotions (grimacing, dissatisfaction). This left three stimuli which were relevant to the question of whether accurate judgments could be made of the infant's emotions. In considering these data, we counted a judgment as correct if it accurately identified the emotion, regardless of whether or not it included a correct identification of the particular eliciting situation. For example, for the photograph taken when the infant had been astonished by the sight of a bright-colored toy, we decided the observers were accurate if they chose that judgment, of if they chose the judgment of "astonishment at the mother counting loudly" or "astonishment while listening to the ticking of a watch." The results were as follows: 94% correct judgments for the astonishment face; 79% correct judgments for the pleasure face; and 21% correct judgments for the fear face. With only one stimulus person and only three relevant stimuli, Goodenough's study was certainly enormously limited, but showed accuracy on two out of three emotions tested.

In another article, Goodenough (1932) reported data she felt contradicted Sherman's. She observed a 10-year-old, blind-deaf child who, because of these handicaps, would have little opportunity to learn facial behaviors. Goodenough dropped a doll inside the child's dress, and described the facial reactions as being similar to the facial behaviors associated with different emotions in normal children. This is interesting anecdotal evidence of an innate tendency to show emotion in the face, but the nature of the data reported limits it to that.

Thompson (1941) and Fulcher (1942) both conducted studies of blind and sighted children, which will be gone over again later in regard to the components of facial behavior (Chapter XVI). Thompson studied spontaneous behavior in 26 blind and 29 sighted children ranging from 7 weeks to 13 years of age; Fulcher studied the posed emotions of 50 blind and 118 sighted children ranging from 4 to 21 years. Both noted maturational factors; both noted, in their analysis of the components of facial behavior, similarities between the blind and sighted children in at least some emotional facial behaviors—*laughing, smiling, crying,* and *anger* for Thompson, and *happiness, sadness, anger,* and *fear* for Fulcher. While differences in the extent of muscular movements were found between blind and sighted children, there was evidence of similarity in the particular muscles moved for each emotion.

Both investigators also utilized a judgment procedure with observers. Thompson had four trained psychologists observe the facial behavior of the blind and sighted children and judge emotion in 11 categories, which she then analyzed in terms of F. Allport's category scheme. There was high agreement among observers, and accuracy in that the emotion judged corresponded with the investigator's impression, based on situational context as well as total behavior shown, for judgments of both blind and sighted children, with no significant differences as a function of sightedness. Fulcher had five observers who knew the intended emotion judge the "adequacy" of the pose. For both blind and sighted children, *happiness* and *sadness* were judged as more adequately portrayed than *anger* and *fear*, but across all emotions the sighted portrayals were judged as more adequate than the blind ones. In discussing their results, Thompson and Fulcher cited Landis and Sherman as providing the main evidence which contradicted their findings.

To summarize our discussion of Sherman's work and related studies, Sherman's evidence for inaccuracy rests upon the presumptions that a different emotion was elicited in each situation, that it was the same emotion for each of the two infants, and that the emotion elicited during the situational manipulation was preserved long enough to appear in the post-elicitation film shown to the observers. These presumptions are of dubious validity. Further, the validity of Sherman's findings can be questioned because of his failure to consider maturational processes and the small size (two) of his sample of stimulus persons. A brief review of studies by Goodenough, Thompson, and Fulcher, all studies of children's facial behaviour which considered blind as well as sighted children, some of which studied different age periods, consistently contradicted Sherman's conclusions.

The Landis and the Sherman experiments, with their questionable negative findings, have, in our opinion, had unmerited influence in the investigation of judgment of emotion from facial behavior. Our lengthy discussion of these studies has been an attempt to set them in perspective. We will turn now to the positive evidence.

The first set of studies (Munn, 1940; Hanawalt, 1944; Vinacke, 1949) used as stimuli photographs drawn from commercial magazines of presumably spontaneous, naturally occurring, emotional behavior. Accuracy was measured in terms of the observers' ability to judge the emotion which presumably occurred in the situation. The second set of studies (Ekman *et al.*, 1964, 1965; Howell & Jorgenson, 1970; Lanzetta & Kleck, 1970) used as stimuli spontaneous reactions elicited in a standard stress interview, spontaneous behavior when anticipating electric shock, and clinical interviews with psychiatric patients. Accuracy was measured in terms of the correspondence between the observers' judgments of emotion and anticipated differences between the stress and catharsis portions of standard interviews and between the pre- and post-hospitalization interviews of psychiatric patients, and between observers' judgments of the eliciting circumstance, shock or non-shock. The last set of studies (Drag & Shaw, 1967; Dusenbury & Knower, 1938; Ekman & Friesen, 1965; Frijda, 1953; Kanner, 1931; Kozel & Gitter, 1968; Levitt, 1964; Osgood, 1966; Thompson & Meltzer, 1964; Woodworth, 1938) used posed behavior as stimuli. Accuracy was measured in terms of the observers' success in judging the emotion intended by the poser.

C. ACCURACY IN JUDGING CANDID PHOTOGRAPHS: MUNN, HANAWALT, AND VINACKE

Munn (1940) explained his decision to have observers judge the emotion shown in magazine photographs, taken during presumably emotional situations, as an attempt to resolve Woodworth's (1938) doubts about whether accuracy was possible for spontaneous as well as posed facial behavior. Munn's primary aim was to determine the influence of knowledge of the situation upon judgment of emotion from facial behavior by comparing the judgments of observers who saw the face alone with those who saw the entire photograph. Though he found that the number of observers making an accurate judgment increased when the entire picture was seen, accuracy was achieved with most of his stimuli even when the face alone was seen. These comparative results will be discussed later in connection with the question of how contextual information influences the judgment of emotion from facial behavior (Chapter XVIII). We will take into account here only Munn's data on the judgments of the face alone.

Hanawalt (1944) borrowed Munn's procedure of utilizing candid photographs from magazines and used a number of Munn's actual stimuli as well as others he gathered himself from magazines. His purpose was not to study accuracy, but to compare judgments made when either the top or bottom half of the face was seen; these results will be considered later in connection with the question of how judgments of emotion are influenced by the components of the face observed (Chapter XVII). Only Hanawalt's results on the judgments of the full face will be considered here.

Vinacke (1949) also drew stimuli from magazines, but chose his own different set of pictures. His purpose was not to study accuracy, but to compare judgments made by different ethnic groups; those results will be scrutinized later in connection with the question of how judgments of emotion may vary across cultures (Chapter XIX). Here we will consider only Vinacke's results on the judgments by Caucasian observers.

Munn recognized that there were difficulties with his two accuracy criteria. He should have sought some means for estimating what emotional reaction was experienced independent of the facial behavior which occurred. He could have approximated that by showing the full photographs, but obscuring the face so that the observer could see only the situation and determine whether there were any agreed upon expectations about the probable emotion.[22] However, he did not do that and, instead, both of his accuracy criteria were contaminated by knowledge of the face as well as knowledge of the situation. One criterion was his own expectation, an unreliable basis, since he was not present when the behavior occurred, and contaminated by his inspection of the faces. The other criterion was the judgment of the observers who saw the situation and the face; it was similarly contaminated, so that it is not possible to know whether their expectation about emotion was influenced primarily by the situation or by their judgment of the face. Neither Hanawalt nor Vinacke concerned himself with accuracy criteria; they analyzed their results solely in terms of observer agreement under the different conditions they employed in their experiments.

The best basis for building an accuracy criterion for use with candid photographs from magazines is not available, precisely because the pictures are selected long after the event with no access to the relevant sources of information, *viz.*, the self-report of the individual, the reports of other people present in the situation, data on the antecedent and consequent events. Though less satisfactory, another basis for establishing an accuracy criterion for such stimulus materials is to determine what single emotion, if any, is usually associated with the situation in which the candid photograph appeared to have been taken. We conducted a simple experiment in which 35 college students were given the list of situations as described by Munn, Hanawalt, and Vinacke (but not any photographs), and were asked to judge the most probable emotion, utilizing the list of proposed emotion categories from Table 2, and also the choice of "no emotion." Only situations yielding at least 50% agreement about a particular emotion were taken to be relevant for examining the accuracy of observers' judgments.[23] Correspondence between

---

[22] This procedure might not be workable if the photographs of the situation did not adequately show what the nature of the setting was, or what the elicitor was, etc. (*see* Chapter II).

[23] The data on 5 of the 14 Munn stimuli were excluded because of lack of agreement about probable emotion, as were the data on 7 of Hanawalt's 20 stimuli and 14 of Vinacke's 20 stimuli.

TABLE 5

Results on Selected Stimuli from Candid Photograph Studies

Verbal Description	Judgment of Verbal Description	Judgment of Face		
		Munn	Hanawalt	Vinacke
Girl Laughing	100 Happy	—	97 Happy	—
Jitterbug Clapping Hands to Music	97 Happy	86 Happy	—	—
Girl Running into Ocean	91 Happy	97 Happy	—	—
A Man Smiling Standing between Two Other Men	88 Happy	—	—	59 Happy
Baseball Fan Vociferously Cheering	82 Happy	—	—	47 Happy
Girl in Sack Race	66 Happy	49 Sad	—	—
Man Escapes Nazis	56 Happy	—	65 Fear	—
Girl Escapes Explosion	53 Happy	—	96 Horror	—
Man in Shower as Water is Unexpectedly Turned on	89 Surprise	—	87 Surprise	—
Girl Discovers Photographer as She Lifts Hoop Skirt to Go through Door	85 Surprise	—	80 Surprise	—
Girl in Amusement Park with Dress Going Up	74 Surprise	—	90 Happy	—
Girl Discovers Photographer Has Her Covered	58 Surprise	—	62 Surprise	—
Girl Photographed over Transom while Dressing	56 Surprise	66 Surprise	89 Surprise	—
Girl Photographed over Transom while in Bath	38 Surprise 12 Fear	26 Surprise 28 Fear	—	—
Girl Running from Ghost	96 Fear	94 Fear	92 Fear	—
Boy Caught in Revolving Door Attended to by Policeman	61 Fear	—	—	1 Fear
Porter Leading Burned Man from Scene of Airplane Crash	56 Fear	8 Fear 33 Anxiety	—	—
Man with Hand Stretched towards Hostile Crowd	54 Fear	63 Distress/ Anxiety	—	—
Frenchman Shows Grief as Colors of Lost Regiment Are Exiled to Africa	79 Sad	—	84 Sad	—
Man Wrapped in Blanket after Failure to Swim English Channel	71 Sad	—	—	4 Sad 16 Exhaustion

TABLE 5 *cont.*

Woman Disheveled Weeping Telephoning	60 Sad	—	—	51 Sad
Girl Sitting in a Police Station after One of Her Suitors Was Killed in a Quarrel over Her Affections	53 Sad	—	—	32 Sad
Man Who Is Holding Strike-breaker by the Coat Collar	68 Anger	8 Anger	65 Anger	—
Lady Awaiting News of Mine Disaster	94 Disgust/ Contempt	—	71 Sad	—

the majority of original judgments of the faces in the photographs and the judgments we obtained of the verbal descriptions of the situations constituted the measure of accuracy. Table 5 gives the verbal description of the situation as it was noted in the articles by these authors and as it was given to our college students, the percentage agreement about the expected emotion made on the basis of reading the verbal descriptions, and the judgments made by the original observers of the face alone. (These last data were reorganized in terms of the categories listed in Table 2, to facilitate comparisons across experiments.)

Accuracy was found with all three sets of data: for 6 of the 9 Munn stimuli listed, for 8 of the 13 Hanawalt stimuli, for 4 of the 6 Vinacke stimuli. The table also shows that this accuracy was achieved with happiness, surprise, fear, and sadness stimuli; the one anger and the one disgust/contempt stimulus yielded either inconsistent or inaccurate results.

The instances of inaccuracy are difficult to explain. Either set of observers could be wrong; or both could be correct if the stimulus person experienced more than one emotion and the camera captured the one which was not normative, or if the stimulus person had an idiosyncratic reaction, or if the verbal description of the situation failed to include relevant information— but that is the limitation of this indirect method of establishing an accuracy criterion.

To summarize, these three experiments show observers can make accurate judgments of spontaneous behavior, in the sense that observers of a face can judge the emotion which other observers who read a description of the situation predict. There are four limitations on these results. First, the behavior studied (candid photographs taken from magazines) may not all actually have been spontaneous. The person shown in the photographs may have been aware of the photographer, or, even worse, might have completely re-enacted or staged the behavior for the press.

The second limitation is the accuracy criterion. Although the one we fashioned (determining what emotion would be expected in the eliciting circumstance), is preferable to the one employed by the original authors, it is still not totally satisfactory for reasons which were discussed above. A third limitation is the sampling of emotions; accuracy was shown for four of the six emotion categories listed in Table 2; the sample for the other two emotion categories was very small, only one stimulus each.

The fourth, and perhaps most serious limitation, is in regard to the representativeness of the findings. Hunt (1941) appropriately noted the need to establish how often facial behavior in situations like those studied by Munn can provide the basis for accurate judgments of emotion. Are informative faces a rare event, usually lost within a sequence of noninformative facial behavior? Or is such informative facial behavior shown only by some special group of people, highly extroverted persons, for example, but not by a more representative sample? Did Munn, or the photographer, pick out the one rare moment, or the few rare people, who happen to provide accurate information in their spontaneous facial behavior? The answers to these questions would require information about sampling which is not available. Information would be needed both from the photographer (how he chose what to photograph and how he selected from among the photographs those which were published), and from Munn, Hanawalt, and Vinacke (how many published photographs they inspected in choosing the particular ones employed in their studies).

While it can be said that accuracy did occur, it is not possible to specify how frequently facial behaviors in situations such as those studied by these authors provide the basis for accurate judgments. Thus, there is doubt about the representativeness of their findings, in terms of *generality across persons* and of *generality across time* within the situation. The next group of experiments to be considered remedies this limitation, but they are weaker than the ones just discussed in that accuracy was sought on gross discriminations rather than on specific emotions.

D. ACCURACY IN THE JUDGMENT OF SPONTANEOUS BEHAVIOR

Let us first note how the design of experiments on spontaneous behavior which we will next examine answers Hunt's criticism of the candid photograph studies, by providing evidence of generality across persons and generality across time. The first question about generality is resolved if there is representative sampling of stimulus persons—that is, if the experimenter does not preselect some atypical group of people who, because of special training, instruction, or proclivity, would be likely to be more facially facile than others. Although there was no information about the sampling of persons in the candid photograph studies, in the studies of spontaneous behavior the sampling of persons was reasonably random within the constraints of utilizing volunteers and the usual sources for subjects. The stimulus persons were either college students or mental patients, but in neither case were good expressors preselected. The number of stimulus persons in each experiment was small; but by considering the finding of accuracy across all of the experiments, this limit is remedied.

The matter of how to design experiments so as to resolve doubts about the generality of the findings across time is more complicated. Let us examine how answers could be furnished to a skeptic who, like Hunt, holds the view that the face rarely emits information which allows for accurate judgment. This skeptic would have no problem in dismissing the candid photograph studies discussed earlier, for there is no evidence on the sampling of behaviors in those studies to counter the skeptic's claim that both photographer and investigator probably chose that one-in-a-million slice of life in which the face happened to show something decipherable and relevant to the eliciting circumstance. If the skeptic is shown evidence of accuracy in an experiment where the investigator did not take a single slice, but showed his observers a continuous sample of some length on film or videotape (Howell & Jorgenson used 60-second samples, Lanzetta & Kleck used 12-second samples), he would have to yield, but only somewhat. The skeptic could no longer claim that the rare moments when facial behavior is informative are usually lost when embedded in the total sequence of random, meaningless facial behavior. If that were so, then observers who saw a sequence would not achieve accuracy. However, he could still argue that only in *rare* moments is the face informative, but rather than being lost, those rare moments provide the basis for accurate judgment. Perhaps one signal in 12 or 60 seconds of facial noise was the basis for accurate judgment, the skeptic would argue, and this provides no evidence that the face often conveys accurate information.

TABLE 6

Methodology and Results of Accuracy Experiments of Spontaneous Behavior

	Ekman 1965	Howell & Jorgenson 1970	Lanzetta & Kleck 1970
Number of Stimulus Persons	5	4	12
Number of Stimuli	60: 12 of each person, half from each of the 2 conditions.	8: two one-minute film clips of each stimulus person, one clip from stress condition, one film clip from relief condition.	—
Type of Record	Still photographs of face, randomly selected from larger record.	Motion picture film of head and shoulders.	12-second videotape of stimulus person while they anticipated shock or nonshock; each observer judged 20 episodes for each of 6 persons.
Number of Observers	35	53	6 observers for each stimulus person
Judgment Task	Ratings on Schlosberg's 3 dimensions: Pleasant-Unpleasant Attention-Rejection Sleep-Tension	Pleasant vs. Unpleasant Dichotomy	Whether the videotape shows shock anticipation trial or nonshock trial.

Sampling Situation	Standardized interview with stressful and cathartic parts.	Standardized interview with stressful and relief parts.	Stimulus persons saw a red light if they were to receive a shock, a green light if no shock on that trial.
Accuracy Criterion	Compare judgments of stimuli from two parts of interview expected to differ in emotion experienced.	Compare judgments with emotions expected in two parts of the interview.	Is judge correct in identifying whether is in shock anticipation (red) or nonshock anticipation (green)?
Results	Median Stress Stimuli: 4.6 Unpleasant Median Cartharsis Stimuli: 5.7 Pleasant	61% Correct Identification	Accuracy significant across stimulus persons observed, although also significant differences among stimulus persons observed. Chance judgment would be 50% correct, and the range across stimulus persons was 55% to 83% correct median of 62%.

TABLE 6 *cont.*

	Ekman & Bressler 1964	Ekman & Rose 1965
Number of Stimulus Persons	10	6
		These 6 patients were also stimulus persons in Ekman & Bressler's study.
Number of Stimuli	40 sequences, each sequence was 5 photos taken in 5 seconds; 4 sequences for each person; half from each of the 2 conditions.	96 sequences, each sequence was 5 photos taken in five seconds; 16 sequences for each person, half from each condition.
Type of Record	5 rapid stills, showing face and body, randomly selected from larger record.	5 rapid stills, showing face and body, randomly selected from larger record.
Number of Observers	34	244
Judgment Task	Ratings on: Pleasant-Unpleasant scale Mobile-Immobile scale	Ratings on: Pleasant-Unpleasant scale Immobile-mobile scale
Sampling Situation	Standardized psychiatric interview with in-patients, two interviews with each patient, one rated as most depressed and one rated as most improved by interviewer.	Standardized psychiatric interview with in-patients, two interviews with each patient, one at time of admission to hospital and one at time of discharge from hospital.
Accuracy Criterion	Compare judgments of stimuli from the two interviews when different emotional experience would be expected.	Compare judgments of stimuli from the two interviews when different emotional experience would be expected.
Results	Median Depressed Stimuli: 3.9 Unpleasant 2.3 Immobile Median Improved Stimuli: 5.1 Pleasant 3.7 Immobile	Median Admission Stimuli: 2.8 Unpleasant 2.9 Immobile Median Discharge Stimuli: 5.0 Pleasant 4.9 Mobile

98

The answer to this remaining claim, that the face is an infrequent output system, requires an experiment in which many separate samples of facial behavior are randomly drawn from within an eliciting situation. If observers are able to make accurate judgments for most of the samples, the skeptic is answered, and representativeness of the findings in terms of generality across time is established. There is one artifact in such a research design which can decrease the probability of obtaining accurate results. Selecting slices of behavior in a random fashion may well fragment the natural flow of behavior. For example, a five-second slice might show the end of one facial behavior and the beginning of another, rather than the beginning, middle, and end of a facial behavior, and increase the difficulty of judging the behavior. Nevertheless in the experiments by Ekman and his associates, randomly drawn multiple samples of behavior did provide the basis for accurate judgments, establishing that the face often provides accurate information, thus answering doubts about generality of findings across time.

Let us now consider this set of experiments. Table 6 shows the methodological features and results of these studies. In some of the studies, the sample of facial behavior was obtained by recording a naturally occurring event; Ekman and Bressler (1964) and Ekman and Rose (1965) used facial behavior shown during interviews conducted at different points in inpatient psychiatric hospitalization. Some utilized a laboratory-contrived situation to elicit emotion; Ekman (1965) and Howell and Jorgenson (1970) used standardized interviews in which the interviewer changed his manner and style; Lanzetta and Kleck (1970) used the anticipation of receiving either a shock or nonshock. Only the studies by Ekman and his associates were designed primarily to study accuracy, but the other studies do provide information relevant to this issue. For all but the Lanzetta and Kleck experiment, the observers who judged emotion knew nothing about either the situation in which the stimuli had been recorded or the nature of the persons photographed.

In the first study listed in Table 6, the accuracy criterion was the expected difference in emotions elicited by the interviewer when he was hostile (stress-inducing) and when he explained the purpose of his hostility and praised the subject for resiliency under stress (catharsis-inducing). The observers rated stimuli from the stressful parts of the interviews as more unpleasant than those from the cathartic parts of the interviews.[24] While the difference in pleasantness rating is small, it is significant, and it should be remembered that these stimuli were selected at random. As mentioned earlier, selecting still

---

[24] There were also significant differences in the ratings on the Attention-Rejection dimension, but these have not been reported since ratings on this scale were highly intercorrelated with ratings on pleasantness.

photographs at random may well fragment the natural flow of behavior, and for that reason provide a low estimate of accuracy. But this random sampling procedure was used because the study was intended to evaluate what the face might show over the course of an entire interview, not what the face might show at its most informative moments. In another study designed to assess the *maximum* accuracy possible, Ekman used as stimuli photographs which observers who saw both face and body had rated as maximally stressful or cathartic. When just the faces of these pictures were shown to another set of observers who judged the pictures on Schlosberg's three dimensions of emotion without knowledge of the interview situation, the difference in pleasantness ratings was large—a mean difference of $3\frac{1}{2}$ points on a 7-point scale.

Howell and Jorgenson (1970) performed an experiment which was very similar in both the eliciting situation and judgment task. Their major interest, however, was in comparing accuracy when the observers saw the face, read or heard the words, or received a combination of sources. We will report here only on their results on the judgment of the facial behavior. Their interviewer changed his behavior from *unfriendly and challenging* to *reassuring*, in order to induce stress and relief from stress. The observers were shown 60 seconds of motion picture film from the stress phase and a 60-second sample from the relief phase and asked to judge whether the person felt pleasant or unpleasant. Despite differences in accuracy achieved for particular stimulus persons and differences in level of accuracy achieved for the relief compared to the stress sample, overall accuracy was found.

Lanzetta and Kleck (1970) focused primarily on the interrelationships among three phenomena—how accurately the stimulus persons' facial behavior could be judged, the GSR indication of psychophysiological arousal during the elicitation, and the stimulus person's performance as an observer of others. We will discuss only the results on accuracy in judging the facial behavior.[25] Stimulus persons were recorded on videotape for 12 seconds while they watched a red light signalling that they would receive shock, or a green light signalling nonshock. The observers were shown the short videotape episodes and required to indicate whether they were watching

---

[25] Lanzetta & Kleck did not attempt to study accuracy but to determine the relationship among an observer's ability to judge facial behavior, the extent to which his own facial behavior could be judged by others, and psychophysiological measures. Their results on these interrelationships are quite interesting, but are not reported here because the authors considered the findings tentative due to the small number of stimulus persons. Their study is quite suggestive, however, that explorations of these variables will be fruitful (*see* also Buck, Savin, Miller & Caul, 1969; Jones, 1950).

the person while he anticipated shock or nonshock. There were 12 stimulus persons; each was judged by five of the other persons and himself. As in the experiment above, accuracy varied with the stimulus person observed, from a low of 55% to a high of 83% correct judgments, with the median accuracy across all stimulus persons observed better than chance, 62%. There are two problems with this experiment as an accuracy study of facial behavior. The videotapes showed more than the face; the body from the waist up was seen, and the observers may have used nonfacial sources for some, or most, of their judgments. Judgment of the eliciting circumstance may or may not have required any information about emotion; perhaps coping behavior provided the basis for accuracy.

The accuracy criterion in the next two experiments was based upon the expected differences in emotions between the acute and remitted phases of a psychotic disorder, confirmed by the ratings of the treatment staff. Ekman and Bressler (1964) found that stimuli randomly selected from interviews of depressive patients during the acute phase of their illness were rated as more unpleasant and more immobile than those selected from the remitted phase. In a replication (Ekman & Rose, 1965), with a larger sampling of stimuli for each person but a smaller number of persons than in the prior experiment, stimuli from the interview closest to the patient's admission to the hospital were judged as more unpleasant and immobile than those from the interview closest to the patient's discharge from the hospital. The mobility ratings were, however, a description of actual movement, not an inference about emotions.[26]

In summary, these five studies consistently showed that observers can accurately judge emotions shown in spontaneous facial behavior, in the sense that their judgments agreed with the emotion expected by virtue of the nature of the eliciting circumstance. This set of studies is particularly important because it establishes that accuracy has generality across persons judged and across time. Through the use of representative sampling of stimulus persons and behaviors, these experiments refute the argument, raised in connection with the candid photograph experiments, that perhaps accuracy is possible for only the rare stimulus person, or the rare moment in time.

The major limitation in these experiments is that the emotion judged was

---

[26] While in both of these studies on depressive patients the body as well as the face was shown in the photographs, there is little likelihood that the observers' judgments of pleasantness could have been based on body cues rather than facial behavior, since in other experiments Ekman (1965b, 1967a) found that observers could not agree in pleasantness judgments when they were restricted to viewing just the body in still photographs.

general rather than specific. Accuracy has been shown only for the distinction between positive and negative emotional states, not for any of the distinctions within those groupings, such as happiness, interest, anger, fear, disgust, etc. The next set of experiments to be explored provides evidence on just this point, showing that accurate judgments are possible for specific emotions. However, we will no longer be dealing with spontaneous behavior, but with posed behavior, and must evaluate the problem of the relevance of posed to spontaneous facial behavior.

E. ACCURACY IN THE JUDGMENT OF POSED BEHAVIOR

Why consider posed facial behavior in a discussion of accuracy? One answer is that there *is* an accuracy question: can an observer viewing a pose accurately judge the emotion intended by the poser? However, if posing is a very special or unique eliciting circumstance, then establishing accuracy in the judgment of poses has little bearing on whether spontaneous facial behavior provides accurate information (*see* discussion of posing, Chapters II and VII). This issue will be addressed after we direct our attention to this set of experiments.

While most investigators of the judgment of emotion from facial behavior have employed as their stimuli posed photographs, only a few presented their data in a manner which allows examination of whether the observers accurately judged the emotion intended by the poser.[27] Most of these studies have methodological problems, many of which can be resolved by considering the findings across all of the experiments.

Table 7 shows both the methodological features and the results of the eight experiments which had as their focus, at least in part, accuracy in the judgment of posed emotions. In the early experiments, the sample both of stimulus persons and of stimuli for each emotion was small; but, as the table shows, these problems were resolved in some of the later studies. Most of the studies used still photographs; three studies used live behavior, a kind of stimulus introducing potential problems (*see* page 50). However, two studies (Levitt, and Kozel & Gitter) used records of sequential behavior (motion picture film), and since their results are broadly comparable to the others, the

---

[27] Frijda (1953) performed an accuracy study which will not be reported since he utilized an admittedly subjective rating of whether the observers had successfully judged the emotions intended or experienced by the two stimulus persons. With both the still photographic presentations and the motion picture film presentations, Frijda concluded that he had demonstrated accurate judgments of emotion.

TABLE 7
Accuracy Studies of Posed Behavior

	Kanner 1931	Woodworth Feleky 1938, 1914	Dusenbury & Knower 1938	Thompson & Meltzer 1964	Levitt 1964	Osgood 1966	Drag & Shaw 1967	Kozel & Gitter 1968	Ekman & Friesen 1965
Number of Stimulus Persons	1	1	2	50	50	50 or *5	48	10	6
Number of Stimuli for Each Emotion	1–3	2	2	100	50	5	10	5	2
Method of Presenting Stimuli	Still	Still	Still	Live	Motion Picture Film	Live	Live	Motion Picture Film	Still
Number of Observers	409	100	388	4	24	110	4	44	57
Number of Judgment Categories Other Than Those Listed Below	**	1	5	2	0	6	3	1	3
Percent Accurate Judgments on:									
Happy	76	93	100	76	86	55	71	86	65
Surprise	75	77	86	—	43	38	68	69	—
Fear	32	66	93	74	58	16	62	80	35
Anger	33	31	92	60	62	39	42	79	—
Sad	66	70	84	52	—	19	49	59	88
Disgust/Contempt	—	74	91	67	45	50	41	55	0
Pleasantness Factor	—	—	—	—	—	0.38***	—	—	—
Intensity Factor	—	—	—	—	—	0.32***	—	—	—
Control Factor	—	—	—	—	—	0.50***	—	—	—

103

* See page 58.
** Kanner allowed free labeling; in reanalyzing his results many of his responses which were not obviously in one of the 6 categories were not verified.
*** These are correlations between intended emotion and observed emotion when the emotion word data were reordered in terms of factor scores.

finding of accuracy is not limited to still photographs. Though earlier studies used only professional actors, and only a selected sample of the presumably best photographs of them, all but one of the studies since 1938 used untrained posers, and all but one of the studies presented all poses, not just the best attempts. (Both exceptions were in the Kozel & Gitter experiment.) Thus, the findings can be said to have generality across a large number of persons, and to a broader range of behavior than might be represented by a preselected photograph of the possibly rare moment when a good pose was emitted. The number of observers is adequate, except in the Thompson and Meltzer and the Drag and Shaw studies, the findings of which are substantially the same as those of the other experiments.

Before considering the results shown in Table 7, a few words of explanation are necessary about particular experiments. Both Kanner's and Woodworth's data are based on judgments of the Feleky posed photographs; and Woodworth's findings are a reanalysis of Feleky's data. Drag and Shaw found significant differences in observer accuracy depending upon whether the male or female posers were judged.[28] But even the most poorly judged group (men) was judged with better than chance accuracy. In the table, we have combined their data for male and female stimulus persons. The Ekman and Friesen (1965) study falls somewhere between posed and spontaneous behavior. Psychiatric patients were asked to show a camera how they were feeling. The patients did not simulate a specified unfelt emotion as in all of the other studies described in Table 7. On the other hand, their facial behavior cannot be taken as spontaneous, since it was occasioned by the investigator's request. Ekman and Friesen asked the patients to describe their feelings in their own words after they had shown their facial expression. Depressive patients were asked to engage in this task at admission to the hospital and again at discharge, since it was expected that they would have different feelings at these two points. The still photographs taken at these two times were shown to observers who did not know that the pictures were of psychiatric patients. The observers utilized the emotion category system proposed by Tomkins (*see* Table 2) to record their judgment of the emotion shown in the photograph. The accuracy criterion was conformity between observer judgment and patient self-description.

---

[28] Recently there have been a few studies which have attempted to isolate some of the variables associated with whether an individual is a well understood or poorly understood emotion poser. The race and sex of the poser have been found to interact with the emotion posed and the race and sex of the observer (Black, 1969; Gitter & Black, 1968; Kozel, 1969), and personality measures and skin conductance have been found related to posing (Buck, Savin, Miller & Caul, 1969).

The results of each experiment reported in Table 7 were reanalyzed in terms of the six emotion categories proposed earlier (Table 2), to facilitate comparison across experiments. Kanner had, himself, subjectively scored his observers' free emotion labels and judgments of the situation; these data were not used, but instead his published raw data were analyzed to provide the results shown in the table. Woodworth himself had recast Feleky's data, which we then further modified in terms of the six emotion categories.

Do these studies show that observers can accurately judge the emotions intended by the posers? Generally, looking across emotions and across experiments, the answer is yes.[29] All of the figures listed are the modal, or most frequent, response to the intended emotion. In all but a few instances the poser's intended emotion was the emotion most frequently perceived by the observers. While the results are far from perfect for any single emotion category across experiments, or for any single experiment across categories, there is certainly more correspondence between intended and judged emotion across these data than might be expected by chance.

It has been customary to dismiss accurate judgments of posed behavior as by and large irrelevant to the question of whether facial behavior is systematically related to emotion and, more specifically, to the study of spontaneous behavior. As we described earlier (Chapters II, III), the argument (*see* Hunt, 1941; Landis, 1924) has been that posed behavior is a specialized, language-like set of conventions or stereotypes which might conceivably be understood, but that by definition such behavior is different from what the face actually does when emotion is spontaneously aroused. As we mentioned in our discussion of eliciting circumstances (Chapter VII), the only direct study of the differences in the components of posed and spontaneous facial behavior was the dubious experiment by Landis, which failed to find any relationship between the face and emotion for either kind of eliciting circumstance.

Indirectly, however, there is considerable evidence that posed behavior is not a specialized, language-like set of conventions unrelated to real emotional behavior. If it were not in some way reflective of emotion, posed behavior in one culture would not be understood by people from different cultures. Later, in exploring cross-cultural studies (Chapter XIX), we will review a large body of data from a number of experiments in which the posed facial

---

[29] In the figures for Drag & Shaw, Dusenbury & Knower, Ekman & Friesen, Kanner, Kozel & Gitter, Thompson & Meltzer, and Woodworth, where there were more emotion categories in the original data than those listed in Table 7, our estimate of accuracy is low, in that the percentages were calculated by dividing the number of correct responses by the total responses to the stimulus including unlisted categories, rather than by dividing by the total number of responses which fit into the six categories.

behavior of Westerners was judged as the same emotion by members of 13 literate cultures and one preliterate culture, and an experiment in which the poses by members of a preliterate culture were accurately judged by members of a literate culture. For these findings to emerge, the behaviors occurring during posing must have developed in the same way across cultures. One reasonable explanation of such development would be that they are in some way based on the repertoire of spontaneous facial behaviors associated with emotion.

We believe that when an investigator asks a subject to pose an emotion he implicitly requests that the person show an extreme, uncontrolled version of the emotion. When the investigator asks for a pose of anger the subject typically will imagine and try to show extreme anger, and will not attempt to deintensify, mask, or neutralize his facial appearance. If the investigator were to ask him to pose an emotion and gave him a low intensity word, such as annoyance, then the subject would attempt to show facial behavior appropriate to moderate or low intensity emotion. It would also be possible to ask the subject to show the facial behavior which would occur if a display rule was operating; e.g., anger at his boss in a situation in which he could not directly manifest his anger. With such an instruction posing might well yield facial behavior which is quite similar to much spontaneous conversational behavior where display rules for the management and control of facial appearance are operative.

If we are correct in our speculation about how the subject typically interprets the posing instruction (*viz.*, as an occasion to display an uncontrolled version of the emotion), then the obtained poses would not be dissimilar from all spontaneous behavior, but would approximate only that spontaneous facial behavior which occurs when a person is not applying display rules to deintensify, mask, or neutralize. However, poses of extreme, uncontrolled emotion may still differ from spontaneous, unmodulated, high-intensity emotion in duration and in complexity of muscle use.

Grouping the results from a number of experiments allows the conclusion that posed facial behavior can be accurately judged, in that the majority of the observers will correctly identify the intended emotion. This result is not limited to expert posers, nor to the best moments in the posing situation, nor to still-photographic representations of posing. The results are limited, however, to the six emotion categories considered. Conceivably, further studies might achieve accurate judgments of poses of other emotions.

F. SUMMARY ON ACCURACY

At the outset of this section, we quoted Bruner and Tagiuri's listing of studies which produced negative and positive evidence on accurate judgments of emotion. Most of the negative studies they cited were irrelevant to the question of accuracy, since those studies utilized drawings rather than real behavior, thus providing only the artist's conception of emotion as the basis for determining correct judgments. The two negative studies on accuracy which remained, those of Landis and of Sherman, were thoroughly criticized, and contradictory findings from other studies were presented to support our contention that these two experiments henceforth should be disregarded.

Contrary to the impression conveyed by previous reviews of the literature that the evidence in the field is contradictory and confusing, our reanalysis showed consistent evidence of accurate judgment of emotion from facial behavior. Without question, the evidence based on posed behavior is far stronger than that based on spontaneous behavior, where a fully adequate study remains to be done. Such a study is needed in order to show accuracy in the judgment of specific emotions in addition to judgment of positive and negative state. There is a need for further study of accurate judgments among the different negative emotions in spontaneous facial behavior. But it seems unnecessary to continue to question whether accurate judgments are possible. More useful research would determine under what conditions, for what kinds of people, in what kinds of roles and social settings, and with what types of accuracy criteria facial behavior provides correct information about emotion; and, conversely, in what kinds of settings and roles, and for what kinds of people facial behavior provides either no information or misinformation.

As we mentioned at the beginning of this chapter, there are two research approaches to the question of whether the face can provide accurate information about emotion. We have considered in this chapter only studies which use the judgment approach, determining whether observers can make accurate inferences about emotion from viewing facial behavior. The success of such studies makes the other approach, the measurement of facial components, quite important. For the judgment studies can only tell us that the information is there, somewhere in the face, and able to be interpreted accurately by observers. The judgment approach cannot tell us *what* facial behaviors are providing this accurate information, what particular muscular movements or wrinkles in the face allow the observer to determine that an individual is in a stressful rather than a cathartic part of an interview, or that an individual is posing anger rather than disgust. To answer these questions, to specify just which facial behaviors are distinctively related to which emotions, we must consider the second approach to the study of accuracy and measurement of facial components, which is the subject of the next chapter.

CHAPTER XVI

Can Measurement of the Components of Facial Behavior Provide Accurate Information?

In component studies facial behavior is the dependent variable or response measure, rather than the independent variable or stimulus as it is in judgment studies. We are not attempting to determine what observers can say about faces, but what the measurement of facial components can indicate about some aspect of a person's experience. In a component study we might ask, for example, "What components of facial behavior differentiate between faces sampled when the subject was afraid and those sampled when the subject was disgusted?" In a judgment study we would ask, "Can observers tell when looking at a face whether the subject was afraid or disgusted?" (the difference between component studies and judgment studies was reviewed earlier, pages 31–33 and page 77).

There have been remarkably few component studies. The scarcity of research is not due to difficulty in establishing independent variables—that is, eliciting circumstances in which to sample facial behavior with some criterion of how the person feels—since these difficulties are also encountered with judgment studies, of which there have been many. Probably it is due to difficulty in deciding what to measure in the face. At this point there is still no accepted notion of the units of facial behavior, nor any general procedure for measuring or scoring facial components. Each investigator has improvised his own techniques, rarely using techniques tried by others and almost invariably combining his facial component units into a few global scores. Three new measurement procedures have very recently been developed, and there is some evidence to support the validity of one of these.

TABLE 8 *Component Studies*

	Landis & Hunt 1939	Trujillo & Warthin 1968	Thompson 1941	Fulcher 1942
Eliciting Circumstances	Experimental presentation of sudden, intense stimuli (primarily .22 pistol shot).	Chronic duodenal ulcer.	Naturally occurring activities. A few stimuli introduced. Emotion inferred from context.	Instruction to pose different emotions.
Emotions Sampled	Startle.	Not specified as emotion.	Laughter, smiling, crying (also isolated inferences of fear and anger).	Anger, fear, happiness, sadness.
Number and Type of Subjects	Normals; also infants, animals, psychotics, epileptics, deaf, patients with neurological disorders, subjects injected with adrenalin, hypnotized subjects.	126 ulcer patients, 274 patients with other medical disorders.	29 seeing children 7 weeks–13 years. 26 blind children 7 weeks–13 years.	118 seeing children 4–16 years. 50 blind children 6–21 years.
Type of Facial Components Measured	Eyeblink, widening of mouth, forward movement of head.	Number of vertical folds between eyebrows.	3-point scale: some/much/no involvement of 8 facial areas.	6-point scale: amount of movement. 6-point scale: amount of distortion (eye and mouth separately). Yes-no judgment of involvement of 18 muscles. 6-point "adequacy" scale.
Results	Strength of response varies directly with intensity and suddenness of stimulus. Some facial response (minimally eye-blink) *always* elicited by stimulus of sufficient strength except in epileptics. Primary pattern shows very little variation	85% of ulcer patients show 3 or more vertical folds, as compared with only 6% of control patients when asked to frown.	Pattern of muscular activity same in blind and seeing for each type of emotional behavior. Seeing subjects show more uniformity of pattern.	More facial activity in seeing subjects. Blind subjects show same general patterns but with less differentiation among emotions.

110

TABLE 8 cont.

	Leventhal & Sharp 1965	Rubenstein 1969	Ekman, Friesen & Malmstrom 1970
Eliciting Circumstances	Pre-childbirth labor, total time in labor divided into 4 intervals.	Depressed patients asked to smile before shock treatment and 1 hour after treatment. Control group of non-patients tested twice.	Each subject watched a neutral travelogue and a stress inducing film of sinus surgery.
Emotions Sampled	"Distress."	"Happiness."	The self-report of the subjects showed that the emotion experienced in the neutral film was slight happiness, and in stress film was interest, surprise, fear, pain, disgust, and sadness.
Number and Type of Subjects	52 women with prior childbirth experience, 19 women with no prior childbirth experience (55 subjects returned Welch anxiety scale, and were divided into high v. low anxious by median split).	17 depressive patients 16 control subjects.	25 college students.
Type of Facial Components Measured	Forehead: 4 behaviors, 2 indices* Brow: 8 behaviors, 3 indices Eyelids: 6 behaviors, 2 indices Nose: 5 behaviors Eyes: 12 behaviors, 2 indices Mouth: 36 behaviors, 3 indices Score: frequency of behavior during 5-minute observation interval.	Amount of development of facial muscles derived from obtaining a series of profile shots taken rapidly on motion picture film within a facial expression.	Facial Affect Scoring Technique measured the presence of fear, anger, surprise, disgust, sadness, happiness. Brow: 8 behaviors Eyes: 17 behaviors Lower Face: 45 behaviors.
Results	Forehead, brow, eyelid indices show increased discomfort (wrinkles, movement) as labor progresses. Other facial indicators insignificant.	More displacement of facial muscles during smile following shock treatment than before; no change from pre- to post- treatment in the control subjects.	More surprise, sadness, disgust, anger in stress than neutral. More happiness in neutral than stress.

111

* Indices of comfort, discomfort (major, minor, or unspecified), change, created by grouping individual behavior measures.

Table 8 summarizes the methodological features and findings from seven studies.[30] All obtained positive results, but each has shortcomings in either interpretation or generality of the results. The Landis and Hunt study detected strong evidence of a specific facial response to a startling stimulus. However, the facial responses they documented for reactions to a sudden noise (a pistol shot) do not resemble the stimuli which observers customarily judged as showing surprise. The startle facial reaction was extremely brief, followed by a secondary reaction, presumably an emotion about the initial startle, which varied across subjects; Landis and Hunt did not determine whether this secondary reaction had systematic properties related to the subjects' reported feelings, or to manipulations in the setting which might have caused the sudden noise to be associated with fear, or interest, or anger.

Trujillo and Warthin's (1968) finding that ulcer patients have more vertical creases in their brow when asked to frown than have other medical patients may or may not be relevant to emotion. They cite Darwin's (1872) and Bell's (1847) notion that the permanent creases in the face result from the most frequently experienced emotions, and on that basis suggest their findings have relevance to emotion. However, they acknowledge that they did not control for chronic pain, and pain is not considered to be an emotion by most authors, although there is evidence (Boucher, 1969) that it does have some distinctive facial components. Their findings, even if relevant to emotion, are too general to be useful, since vertical creases in the brow can be found with anger, fear, or sadness, and they did not examine other facial components which might further distinguish between these emotions.

Leventhal and Sharp's (1965) findings are open to similar questions about whether facial components of pain or of some specific emotion during childbirth are responsible for their results. They use Tomkins' term "distress" to describe the emotion they studied. Earlier (pages 61–62), we pointed out that the term is problematical in that it can refer either to sadness-grief, or to pain-hurt-suffering. Their discomfort indices, built from scores on the eyebrows, forehead, and eyelids, may well have measured either pain or sadness,

---

[30] Landis also conducted a component study on the same materials he showed to observers, and failed to find any components related to his eliciting circumstances or the subjects' self-report. His results will not be discussed, both for the reasons already outlined (Chapter XV), which raise serious doubts about his study, and because of two additional problems relevant to his components analysis. In computing the participation of the various muscles, he included pictures taken before and after the actual eliciting stimuli; to what extent the ubiquitous nervous smile he refers to is a function of including one "expectancy" situation (the before-elicitation pictures) with every situation cannot be gauged. And, in analyzing his data, Landis used a technique that was both extremely conservative (Frois-Wittmann) and inappropriate for the problem (Davis).

or both. Their study is noteworthy, however, in that their facial behavior measures were related not only to severity of labor, but to number of previous births and to anxiety.

Both Fulcher (1942) and Thompson (1941) analyzed their results primarily by comparing blind with sighted children, and reported their data in a way which makes it difficult to determine what the precise differences in the facial components were for each emotion they studied, within either sample of children. Yet, they both reported more extensive lists than most other investigators of facial components which they hypothesized as distinctive for each emotion. Thompson's results on smiling, laughing, and crying showed similarities in the distinctive movements of the facial components for each of these reactions for her blind and sighted subjects. Less information is provided about anger and sadness, although she said they also had distinctive facial components in both blind and sighted children. Fulcher's study of the posed emotions of blind and sighted children provides information on a wider sampling of emotions, and with more information about the distinctive components for each emotion, but not in sufficient detail to check his hypotheses about whether the components of facial behavior are distinctive for each emotion posed. His findings do suggest that facial components unique to each posed emotion could be isolated and measured, and it is surprising that there have not been other studies on this question utilizing the posing procedures with sighted adults or children.

Rubenstein's procedure for measuring facial components is novel but quite cumbersome. A 16 mm motion picture camera is rotated around the subject's face rapidly, acquiring a series of profile frames during a facial expression. His method of recording requires, however, that the subject freeze an expression for at least five seconds while the camera travels around the face, and that the subject be in a rather immobilized position. This procedure is not only questionable in terms of its applicability to spontaneously occurring facial behavior, but the subjects are constantly made aware that their facial behavior is of interest. His finding that depressive patients smile more broadly when asked to do so after shock treatment than before does demonstrate that his measurement procedure works, but it adds little information about the facial components.

The most elaborate, complex, and promising study is a recent experiment by Ekman, Friesen, and Malmstrom (1970). We will report this experiment in some detail because of its complexity, the import of the findings, and the relevance of the methods and results to our discussion in two later chapters, and also because the findings are so recent that they have not been previously reported in the literature. (This work is reported in Ekman, 1972.)

In conjuction with Averill, Opton, and Lazarus, Ekman and his associates collected records of the facial behavior, skin resistance, heart rate, and self-reported emotion of subjects in the U.S. and Japan, as they watched a neutral and a stress film. We will discuss here only their findings on the facial behavior of the American subjects; in Chapter XIX we will discuss the cross-cultural comparison with Japanese subjects.

This study utilized a new tool for measuring facial behavior, *viz.*, Ekman, Friesen, and Tomkins' Facial Affect Scoring Technique (FAST). The derivation of this technique, and the details of its use are reported elsewhere (Ekman, Friesen, & Tomkins, 1971), but it will be necessary to provide some information about how the scoring procedure was used in order to explain the findings and convey something about the comprehensiveness of this measurement system. We will first describe the use of FAST, and then the experiment in which it was used, explaining the results which are listed in Table 8.

FAST requires scoring of each observable movement in each of three areas of the face: (1) brows/forehead area; (2) eyes/lids; (3) lower face, including cheeks, nose, mouth, chin. Rather than defining each scoring category in words, FAST employs photographic examples to define each of the movements within each area of the face which, theoretically, distinguish among six emotions: happiness, sadness, surprise, fear, anger, and disgust. For example, instead of describing a movement as "the action of the frontalis muscle which leads to raising of both brows in a somewhat curved shape, with horizontal wrinkles across the forehead," FAST utilizes a picture of just that area of the face in that particular position to define that scoring item. Figure 1 shows as an example the items across facial areas that are considered to be relevant to surprise.

FAST is applied by having independent coders view each of the three areas of the face separately, with the rest of the face blocked from view. It should be emphasized that the FAST measurement procedure does *not* entail having the coder judge the emotion shown in the face he is coding. Rather, each movement within a facial area is distinguished, its exact duration determined with the aid of slowed motion, and the type of movement classified by comparing the movement observed with the atlas of FAST criterion photographs. If, for example, the coder is looking at the brows/forehead, and sees a particular movement in that area of the face, he compares the movement with the 8 photographs of brow/forehead movements in the FAST atlas, and assigns to it the FAST atlas number of the criterion picture it most closely resembles. In addition to those for the brows, there are 17 criterion photographs of eyes/lids, and 45 criterion photographs of the lower face in the FAST atlas.

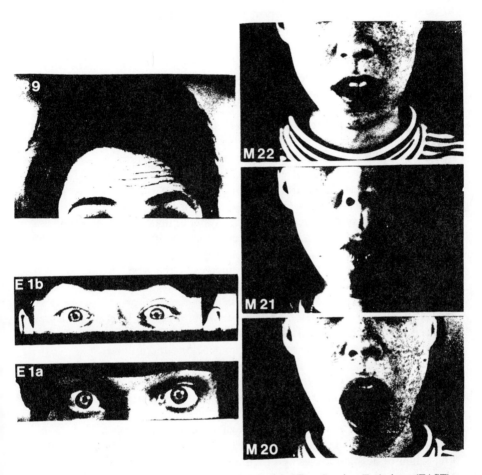

Fig. 1. Examples of criterion items from the Facial Affect Scoring Technique (FAST) showing the brow/forehead, the eyes/lids and the lower face items for surprise.

Once scoring has been completed by the coders, formulas are used to derive the emotion prediction for each facial movement, taking account of the scoring of more than one independent coder. For example, if the facial movement is coded by more than one coder as most closely resembling the FAST brow/forehead picture B9 (shown in Fig. 1), then that movement is labeled surprise. The output of the scoring system is a series of duration scores for anger, fear, surprise, sadness, disgust, and happiness for the brows/forehead, for the eyes/lids, and for the lower face.

Data analysis can be performed by measuring either the *frequency* of occurrence of each emotion within each facial area, or the *duration* for each emotion within each facial area. The frequency or duration scores can be analyzed separately for each of the three facial areas, or emotion scores for the total face can be obtained by utilizing another formula which combines the scores for emotions shown across the face into a total face score for a single emotion or a blend of emotions. In the results reported in Table 8, total face scores were calculated only for a movement which had occurred in at least two of the three facial areas, and only for single emotions.

With a scoring system such as FAST, a system intended to measure facial behavior which distinguishes among six emotions, the question must be raised as to whether or not it is valid. There are two types of validity, which we may call *personal* validity and *social* validity. In the next chapter we will present the results of a study of FAST's social validity—whether measures of facial behavior can predict how people will judge the emotion shown in a face. In this chapter we have been discussing personal validity—whether measures of facial behavior can provide accurate information about the person, that is, about some aspect of his emotional experience or circumstance.

Let us turn now to the question asked in the Ekman, Friesen, and Malmstrom experiment. Can the measurement of facial behavior accurately distinguish whether subjects watched a stressful or a neutral motion picture film?

In the data pool collected jointly by Ekman and his associates and by Averill, Opton, and Lazarus, each subject had been seated alone, watched first a film of autumn leaves and then a three-minute stress-inducing film of sinus surgery. Unknown to the subjects, a videotape record was made of their facial behavior. Subsequently, the subjects answered a questionnaire about their emotional experience during the stress film. The FAST scoring system was applied to every observable movement in each of the three areas of the face, for the 25 American subjects; approximately three minutes of their facial behavior during the neutral film and three minutes during the stress film were scored.

The results revealed an enormous difference in the facial behavior shown in these two eliciting circumstances. The total face scores, the scores for each of the separate facial areas, the scores based on frequency, and the scores based on duration, all indicated that there was more behavior which FAST described as *surprise, sadness, disgust,* and *anger* shown during the stress film, and more behavior which FAST measured as *happiness* shown during the neutral film.

This study shows that measurement of facial behavior accurately discriminates between two eliciting circumstances, watching a neutral and a stress film. Importantly, this difference between facial behavior shown in two different eliciting circumstances was obtained with a measurement system designed to measure six different emotions, rather than being limited to the occurrence of one or two emotions, or to the distinction between positive and negative feelings.

The experiment was not designed to provide evidence that FAST can accurately indicate each of the six emotions it was designed to measure. The only accuracy criterion available is the two film conditions, stress and neutral. Although self-reports were gathered, they are a poor accuracy criterion in this experiment because while the stress film appears to have elicited different emotions in each subject, the self-report did not provide any information about the sequence of emotions experienced, and the self-report data were gathered some time after the experience. What is required is to obtain a self-report on the felt emotion immediately after a particular facial behavior occurs; such a study is in progress.

There are two other sources of information which imply that FAST does succeed in accurately differentiating particular emotions. In Chapter XIX we will discuss the high correlations between the specific emotions shown by American and Japanese subjects as measured by FAST. While it cannot be said from those findings that FAST accurately measured each emotion, it can be said that FAST differentiated types of facial behavior, and that these different types of facial behavior occurred with the same frequency in subjects from two different cultures who were placed in the same eliciting circumstances. For example, even though we cannot conclude that there is evidence that the FAST scores for "disgust" do actually measure disgust, and those for "surprise" do actually measure surprise, it is encouraging that the FAST measurements show the same ratio of "disgust" to "surprise" behavior across members of two cultures who were subject to the same eliciting circumstance.

The last piece of evidence which suggests that FAST can accurately measure specific emotions comes from a study to be outlined in the next chapter, on the social validity of FAST. In that experiment FAST scores accurately forecast the specific emotions which were judged by those who simply observed the face.

One reason why we have described Ekman, Friesen, and Malmstrom's experiment at some length is because of the importance, in our view, of research which directly measures facial components. There has been too little of such research. While judgment studies in which observers tell us their impressions about a face can be quite informative, they cannot provide knowledge about the specific facial behaviors which relate to specific emotions, and many of the questions which need to be answered about the face and emotion cannot be approached solely through the use of judges. Most investigators have avoided direct measurement of facial components, and the few who did measure facial behavior, discussed earlier in this chapter, did not offer a general tool for measuring the occurrence of a number of different emotions. Ekman, Friesen, and Tomkins' FAST is intended as a general-purpose tool to measure the occurrence of six different emotions, and blends of those six. In work in progress they are also developing FAST scores for contempt and interest.

Two other scoring systems for measuring facial behavior have recently been developed by investigators following an ethological approach, Blurton-Jones (1969) and Grant (1969). Neither has yet performed any validity studies. All three systems, FAST and those developed by Blurton-Jones and Grant have considerable overlap, although they differ in a number of regards. FAST is based upon theory, attempting to specify only those facial behaviors which can distinguish one emotion from another, while the other two systems have attempted inductively to derive a descriptive system to cover all facial behavior which they had observed in their samples of adults or children. The scoring items are depicted in terms of a photographic atlas in FAST, while the other two systems utilize a verbal description of particular muscular movements and wrinkles. The appearance of these three scoring systems is an exciting development, offering investigators a choice where there was recently none for measuring the face.

SUMMARY

The few studies on components of facial behavior are encouraging, suggesting that accurate information about some aspect of a person's experience (whether it be response to a gun-shot, to child-birth, to a stress-inducing film) can be derived from measures of facial components; but much more work is needed to supply a definitive answer as to whether measurements of the face can provide accurate information about specific emotions. The evidence to date is limited to showing that accurate information about the distinction between positive and negative emotional reactions can be obtained from measurements of the face.

We believe this is one of the most crucial areas for further research, and that the ability to measure the face directly, rather than solely relying upon observers' global judgments, will be the key to a breakthrough in the next generation of questions about the face and emotion. (Chapter XXI lists some of these next-generation questions.) There are now three alternative scoring systems for measuring the face, and for one of these, Ekman, Friesen, and Tomkins' FAST system, there is partial but very encouraging evidence of validity.

CHAPTER XVII

Are Components of Facial Behavior Related to Observers' Judgments of Emotion?

Studies designed to determine what facial components provide the observer with information about emotion differ from those reviewed in the last chapter. While those relate facial measurements to some accuracy criterion, these relate measurements to the observer's judgment of emotion, regardless of whether the judgment is correct. That is to say, rather than relating facial components to some aspect of the experience of the person who showed the facial behavior, here we relate facial measurements to the observers' interpretations of the stimulus person's face. Although our discussion is limited to the judgment of *emotion*, this is more broadly a question of person perception. What connections are there between particular physical aspects of one person (various facial components) and the perceiver's impressions of him (judgment of emotion)?

The major obstacle to all research on facial components, regardless of whether such measurements are related to accuracy or to observers' judgments, is the problem of determining just what aspect of facial behavior should be measured. What are the size and number of the component units, and how can they be quantified? In most of the studies relating components to observers' judgments, this difficult issue has been bypassed. The investigators did not directly measure facial components but, instead, limited the area of the face which the observer could see. Inferences about the importance of facial components (e.g., horizontal wrinkles) within particular areas (e.g., forehead) were made by comparing judgments made from one facial area with judgments made from another. We will consider these studies of facial *areas* first, and then discuss the few studies which directly measured facial *components*.

A. JUDGMENT AS A FUNCTION OF FACIAL AREA OBSERVED

In all but one of seven studies, the judgments of observers who saw only part of the face were compared with the judgments of observers who saw either another part of the face or the whole face. A question asked in such studies is whether a specific emotion (e.g., happiness) or even all emotions might be better judged from one facial area than from another. Even when successful, such studies do not provide information about the particular facial components relevant to the judgment of a particular emotion, but they do delimit the location of such components. The most popular division of facial areas has been the top (including the eyes) from the bottom. In a few studies three or four divisions have been made, and Frois-Wittmann was the first to note that anatomical possibilities for independent movements of the facial muscles argue against a simple dichotomy of facial areas.

All of the experiments suffer from severe methodological handicaps. No study had a sufficient sampling of stimulus persons, of behaviors of each person, of eliciting circumstances, or of emotions to justify any conclusions; and each study utilized somewhat different judgment tasks and methods for presenting stimuli. We will not provide any tables summarizing methods or results, because our inspection and reanalysis of the data did not suggest interpretations different from the authors', and considering results across the set of seven does not resolve methodological problems or suggest any common findings. Two authors discovered evidence for the superiority of the mouth area (Ruckmick and Dunlap), two found evidence of no reliable differences between facial areas (Frois-Wittmann and Coleman), and three provided evidence that the importance of facial area depended upon the particular emotion judged (Hanawalt, Nummenmaa, and Plutchik).

Ruckmick (1921) performed the first study in which observers saw either the top or bottom half of the face. Posed facial behavior of one stimulus person was employed, and the judgments of the bottom half of the face were found to be more similar to the judgments of the full face than were judgments of the top half. The data were not reported, so it was not possible to verify these results. Dunlap (1927) reported similar findings. He sampled facial behavior in laboratory situations similar to those used by Landis. Observers were given four photographs at once, two of which were composites of the top and bottom halves of the other two. The observers' task was to select the original which most resembled each composite. He found that the bottom half of the face dominated in the sense that the composites were usually judged as most similar to the original which shared the same bottom. But, acknowledging that his eliciting circumstances were not completely successful, many of his photographs were of poor quality, and the composites difficult to make, he restricted his conclusion to the importance of the mouth as a clue for the judgment of happiness.

Frois-Wittmann (1930) showed the top of the face to one group of observers and the mouth area, excluding the nose and cheeks, to another. The observers were told to choose a single word from a list of 43 emotion terms. The stimuli were posed photographs of himself and drawings made from these photographs. Comparing judgments of the whole face with those of the top or mouth, he concluded that there was "no consistent dominance of either eyes or mouth in the determination of the judged expressions of the face." Coleman (1949), utilizing quite different eliciting circumstances, came to the same conclusion. The stimuli were motion picture films of two subjects' facial behavior during eight spontaneous situations similar to those employed by Landis and Dunlap, and of the subsequent posed behavior of remembered reactions to the eight situations. Observers saw the top, bottom, and whole face, with the judgment task requiring that they select the correct eliciting circumstance from a list. He concluded, "in general, identifications of the facial expressions of emotion were not made more reliably from either the mouth region or eye region. The identifiability of a specific facial expression of emotion was found to be dependent upon the subject, the facial region viewed, and whether or not the expression was acted or natural."

Hanawalt (1944) compared observers' judgments of emotion from top, bottom, or whole face versions of candid magazine photographs and of Ruckmick's posed faces. His evidence on judge agreement suggested that the area of the face most likely to elicit judgments similar to those for the whole face depends upon the emotion. For both his candid and posed pictures, the bottom of the face was better judged from the top on *happiness*, while the top was better judged on *surprise*, *anger* and *fear*; the results on *sadness* were equivocal. His results, like those of Coleman and Frois-Wittmann, did show marked differences between areas of the face for particular stimuli.

Nummenmaa's (1964) findings partly contradicted Hanawalt's. Nummenmaa had an actor attempt to pose three "pure" emotions (happiness, surprise, and anger), and blends of each of the pair combinations. Different groups of observers were shown the forehead, the eyes, the nose, or the mouth and were asked to judge the presence of a single emotion, or any of the emotion pair blends, or the blend of all three. Because there were only two stimuli for each of the intended emotions, "pure" or blend, of only one actor, the results must be treated with considerable caution. Inspection of the stimuli themselves suggests to us that this actor was rather atypical in not utilizing brow/forehead movements.

High agreement (70%) for happiness was obtained with the eyes and nose but not the mouth or brow. This contradicts Hanawalt's and Dunlap's findings on the mouth, but because they treated the mouth as part of the bottom of the face, while Nummenmaa separated the mouth from the nose, the difference in results is difficult to explain. High agreement (97%) on surprise was found only for the mouth, contradicting Hanawalt's findings for the top half of the face. Anger was judged with high agreement both on the eyes (67%) and on the mouth (73%). The presence of blends was judged with moderate agreement (between 40–56% with a choice among seven categories) from each area of the face, for at least one of his stimuli. However, often the stimulus judged as a blend when seen in whole-face version was judged as either of the two separate emotions involved in the blend when the separate areas were seen. Nummenmaa interpreted his findings as showing that the eyes were the only region which usually conveyed to the observers the presence of both of the blended emotions.[31] Considerable caution is necessary about Nummenmaa's interpretation of his findings. As mentioned before, there were only a few stimuli from the poses of only one person, who perhaps displayed a less than usually active brow. Further, the data suggest that for half of the intended blend stimuli, the actor failed in the sense that less than half of the observers judged a blend when they saw the full face. If only those stimuli are considered which did convey a blend to the majority of the observers when the full face was seen, then there is no difference in frequency of blend judgment as a function of the area of the face observed. Nummenmaa's results have importance, however, in suggesting that it may be possible to show that components of facial behavior will differentiate not only among single emotions, but also among particular blends.

The last study to be considered can only be described generally, since Plutchik (1962) provided little information about the stimuli and only summarized the results. Two actors attempted to show all possible movements of the face, without concern for associated emotions. Still photographs presenting only one area of the face were shown to observers, who judged them with Plutchik's set of emotion categories. Translating his terminology into the category scheme proposed in Table 2, the mouth was most important for *happiness, anger,* and *disgust*; the eyes for *fear* and *sadness*; eyes, mouth, and

---

[31] We are tempted to interpret this finding as due to the fact that the eye area is responsive both to movements in the brow (upper eyelid) and to movements of the nasolabial fold of the cheek (lower lid and wrinkles near the outer corner of the eye); thus if the brow were to show the components for one emotion, and the mouth area the components for another emotion, it might well be that the eye would reflect in wrinkle patterns the operation of the diverse muscular movements above and below.

forehead for *surprise*. In a parallel experiment, he presented the partial faces to other observers who were asked to compose a face for each emotion from the partial faces. He reports that *happiness* and *sadness* have a neutral brow/forehead; *surprise*, *fear*, and *disgust* have raised foreheads, while *anger* is depicted with a frowning forehead. In regard to the eyes, he did not report the distinctive components, but noted overlaps between particular emotions: *surprise* and *fear*, *disgust* and *anger*. In regard to the mouth, *sadness* and *anger* were said to be most similar.

In sum, these seven studies of how observers' judgments of emotion might vary with the area of the face observed have yielded contradictory results. Every finding was contradicted by at least two other investigators. We believe this confusion is due to an oversimplified view of how facial components might be related to emotion, based on an unwarranted assumption that different facial areas are independent, and a questionable assumption that there is one movement in one facial area for each emotion.

Earlier (*see* Footnote 31), we mentioned our impression that the area of the eyes will often reflect the action of muscles in other areas of the face: brow/forehead, nose, mouth, and cheek/nasolabial fold. This is not always the case; some eye movements do not anatomically cause changes in other areas of the face, and some movements in other areas of the face do not anatomically cause changes in the appearance of the eyes. But strictly on the basis of anatomy, completely apart from habitual linkages between movements in different muscle areas, the facial areas are not as independent as most of the studies have presumed.

Perhaps more important, it seems doubtful that there is only one movement in only one area of the face for each emotion. Instead, we believe that for *each* emotion there may be a number of alternative movements within *each* facial area. Some of these alternatives may lead an observer to an emotion-specific judgment, some may permit him to narrow the choices to two or three emotions, with inspection of other areas further narrowing the choice.

The facial areas may differ in terms of the numbers of alternative components within each area which are relevant for each emotion. A further complication is that there are a number of facial movements within each facial area which are completely irrelevant to emotion. The face is not simply a display system for emotion. There are facial gestures (winks, sticking out the tongue, etc.) and instrumental actions (yawning) of the face which are not specific to any one or two emotions. The facial areas probably differ in terms of the ratio of nonaffective movements to affect-specific components which can occur. The brows/forehead probably have a smaller number of non-affective movements and also of affect-specific components than the lower face. In both spontaneous and posed eliciting circumstances, there is probably considerable variability across persons, and perhaps even within the performance of a particular person. As a consequence, alternative affect-specific components will be shown for the same emotion, and variation in the involvement of components across different facial areas will occur. For example, observers may be able to agree that a face shows anger if the brows are drawn together and lowered and the rest of the face is not active. But they may also judge a face as angry when there is activity in the lower face, such as pressing the lips firmly together, or even when an open square mouth is shown.

If our reasoning is correct, then the confusion in results would be dissipated only by a better definition of separate facial areas, and by sampling a very large number of persons and stimuli. The actual specification of facial components, and the correlation of these with judgments of the whole face, may actually be a shorter research route than studies of judgments of different facial areas. We shall now turn to consider such studies of facial components, which support some of the hypotheses we have just made about alternative components in each facial area for each emotion.

B.   RELATIONSHIP BETWEEN OBSERVERS' JUDGMENTS AND MEASURES OF FACIAL COMPONENTS.

The studies we will consider each utilized a different procedure, asked somewhat different questions, and obtained some promising results. Frijda and Philipszoon (1963) asked whether measures of facial components would be correlated with observers' dimension judgments. Frois-Wittmann (1930) asked which facial components were unique and which were shared across emotion categories. Ekman, Friesen, and Tomkins (1971) asked whether their coding system for scoring facial components would predict the emotion category judged by the majority of observers. All three were limited to measuring facial components in still photographs of posed behavior. Two of the three were further limited by having only one or two stimulus persons; the third, that of Ekman, Friesen, and Tomkins, had 28 stimulus persons, quite a large sample.

Frijda and Philipszoon (1963) had 30 whole-face photographs of an actress judged by 12 observers on 27 bipolar scales. Frijda (1968a) had 48 photographs of another actress (Marjorie Lightfoot) judged by an unreported number of observers on 28 bipolar scales. Factor analysis of these ratings yielded roughly the same five factors for both stimulus persons. The photographs of each stimulus person were scored on 29 facial components by three to five persons. These 29 scores were then combined into 11 global scores. Correlations were calculated between the 11 facial component scores and the five factor scores from the observers' judgments of each of the two stimulus persons. Each of the facial scores correlated significantly with usually just one of the five factors derived from the observers' judgments. But more than half of these correlations were found for only one of the two stimulus persons. If we consider only those which correlated significantly for both stimulus persons, the findings are as follows:

Facial Component	Factor
Smiling/Laughter and Frowning	Pleasantness
Tension	Natural-Artificial
Expressiveness, muscular activity and mouth open/closed	Intensity Factor
Muscular Activity, eyes open/closed	Attentional Activity

No facial component score was correlated for both stimulus persons with the surprise factor.

Frijda is not explicit about how he arrived at his original list of 29 facial component scores, nor does he describe his criteria for combining them into his 11 composite measures. His composite measures cannot be considered an exhaustive consideration of the facial features, and he considered each of those 11 measures singly, without taking account of affect-specific combinations of facial components, as do Frois-Wittmann and Ekman, *et al.* His conclusion, that "much of expressive meaning, in terms of these factors, remains unpredictable on the basis of the facial features" (1968a), seems unwarranted.

Frois-Wittmann (1930) utilized 227 stimuli, divided about equally between photographs of himself and drawings made from these photographs, and between whole and partial faces.[32] Unfortunately, he reported his data on the measurement of facial components in a way which does not allow determination of which results pertain to the drawings and which to the photographs, which to the whole faces and which to the partial faces. Each stimulus was

---

[32] Although we have not considered results previously in which the investigator used drawings of the face, we have made an exception for Frois-Wittmann because the drawings were not the imaginings of an artist but direct tracing from photographs, and because half of the results reported were obtained on actual photographs as well.

judged by from 15 to 120 observers, who employed a list of 43 emotion terms. (We have reorganized his judgment data into the six categories of emotion proposed in Table 2.) Each stimulus was also scored for the absence or presence of 22 facial components; (he did not report his basis for choosing those facial units). Table 9 shows the 22 facial components and indicates those components which were found for at least 80% of the photographs judged to represent a particular emotion category. Frois-Wittmann noted that only a few facial components were specific to only one emotion category; a number of pairs of components occurring jointly were specific to one emotion category; further, more complex permutations differentiated stimuli assigned to one emotion category from those assigned to another. He also found that the number of facial components shared by a pair of stimuli was a good indicator of the amount of judgment confusion between emotion categories. Frois-Wittmann interpreted his data as contradicting the notion that for each emotion there is but one muscular component; he concluded that "the significance of a muscular involvement is therefore not constant, but relevant to the rest of the pattern, for it is always conditioned by the influence exercised on each muscular involvement by all the muscular involvements of the face."

Drawing conclusions from Frois-Wittmann's results is difficult, for the following reasons: only one stimulus person was used, and the results were combined for partial and full faces, for drawings and photographs; no determination was made of whether facial components might be better related to stimuli which elicited high agreement than to those which elicited low agreement about emotion. His results have importance, however, in showing that a procedure for measuring facial components can yield relationships to observed emotion if the pattern of components across facial areas is considered. It is hard to explain why Frois-Wittmann's study has had so little influence. Though Coleman and Hanawalt each cited his findings, they did not profit from his argument and findings against dividing the face into top and bottom areas. Similarly Frijda and Philipszoon apparently did not attend to Frois-Wittmann's findings suggesting the necessity to consider combinations of components rather than each component separately. Most surprising is that his quite early study which found evidence that facial components were related to judgments of emotion led to so little other research along these same lines.

Ekman, Friesen, and Tomkins' (1971) study utilized Frois-Wittmann's findings, although they pursued a somewhat different question, utilizing different methods. In the last chapter, we reported their use of the Facial Affect Scoring Technique (FAST) in an accuracy study in which FAST scores successfully differentiated facial behavior shown during the watching of a

Frois-Wittmann's Results on the Muscle Involvements Occurring in at Least 80% of the Stimuli for Each of Six Emotions

Feature	Judged Emotion*					
	Happy N=22	Surprise N=32	Fear N=27	Anger N=32	Sad N=31	Disgust N=37
Brow: frown or raised	—	—	raised: 92	frowning: 100	frowning: 100 raised: 83	—
Upper Lid: raised or depressed	depressed: 87	raised: 91	raised: 96	raised: 100	—	—
Lower Lid: wrinkled	wrinkled: 100	—	—	wrinkled: 93	—	wrinkled: 86
Nostrils: pinched or dilated	dilated: 90	—	—	dilated: 88	—	—
Lips: open or closed	open: 82	open: 100	open: 100	open: 92	—	—
Teeth: exposed upper or lower and open or closed	—	open: 95	open: 96	lower teeth exposed: 92	—	closed: 94
Upper Lip: raised, depressed or protruding	—	—	—	—	—	raised: 97
Lower Lip: raised, depressed, or protruding	—	—	—	depressed: 92	—	—
Corners of Mouth: raised, retracted, or depressed	raised: 82 retracted: 94	—	—	—	depressed: 90	—

*N equals the number of photographs in each emotion category.

129

stress-inducing film from facial behavior while watching a neutral film. We will consider now their use of FAST to predict the social value of a face, i.e., what emotion observers would judge when they viewed a face. The reader is referred to the previous chapter (pages 114–116) for a description of the FAST system. Unlike Frijda's and Frois-Wittmann's measurement of facial components, Ekman, Friesen, and Tomkins employed pictorial rather than verbal definitions of facial components for use in their measurement procedure.

Whole face photographs which were thought likely to convey a single emotion were shown to a group of observers, and also separately scored on FAST. Eighty pictures were drawn from the photograph sets of a number of investigators and shown to 82 observers who were allowed to indicate the presence of one or two emotions from a list of six. Fifty-one of these stimuli (ten each for *happiness*, *sadness*, *anger*, and *surprise*, seven for *fear* and four for *disgust*) met the criteria established to ensure that these stimuli conveyed only one emotion to the observers.[33] These 51 pictures included photographs of 28 different stimulus persons, at least seven different persons for five of the six emotion categories (disgust being the exception with four), with at least one photograph from the sets developed by Frois-Wittmann, Frijda, Izard, Nummenmaa, Schlosberg, Tomkins, and Ekman and Friesen.

Each photograph was scored with the FAST procedure by masking it to reveal only one facial area and comparing it with the FAST criterion photographs for that facial area. It should be remembered that the FAST scoring system is composed of photographic examples of each facial component relevant to emotion in each of three facial areas (*see* page 114, Chapter XVI). Three coders independently scored the 51 pictures. Each facial area received as its emotion category score the FAST criterion photograph it most closely resembled. The emotion predicted for the photograph was the emotion associated with the FAST criteria for the majority of the three facial areas; i.e., if a photograph had been scored as being most similar to one of the brow/forehead FAST criterion photographs which were to represent components for sadness, and as being most similar to one of the eye area FAST criterion photographs designed to represent fear, and as most similar to one of the FAST criterion mouth/nose/chin/nose photographs designed to

---

[33] The 80 photographs included all which past studies had shown to elicit more than 70% observer agreement about a particular emotion category, and others which had not been used in a judgment study but were anticipated on inspection to yield high observer agreement about a specific emotion category. The criteria for selecting single-emotion photographs were that the photograph be assigned to one emotion category by at least 70% of the observers for their first choice, and that the observers recording the presence of any blend be fewer than 40%.

TABLE 10

Ekman, Friesen, & Tomkins' Fast Prediction of Emotion Judged by the Majority of Observers

Emotion Judged by Majority of the Observers	Fast Prediction In Terms of Majority Score Across 3 Facial Areas										
	Happiness	Surprise	Anger	Sadness	Disgust	Fear	Hapiness Surprise	Fear Sadness	Fear Surprise	Sadness Surprise	No Prediction
Happiness	9	—	—	—	—	—	1	—	—	—	—
Surprise	—	10	—	—	—	—	—	—	—	—	—
Anger	—	—	10	—	—	—	—	—	—	—	—
Sadness	—	—	—	9	—	1	—	—	—	—	—
Disgust	—	—	—	—	3	—	—	—	2	—	1
Fear	—	1	—	1	—	3	—	—	—	—	—

represent sadness, then the prediction would be that the photograph would be judged sad by the majority of the observers who saw the photograph.

Table 10 shows that the FAST scores predicted the observers' judgments on 44 of the 51 photographs. Perfect prediction was obtained with the *surprise* and *anger* stimuli, and there was only one error each on *sadness* and *happiness* photographs. One incorrect prediction was made on the *disgust* pictures, and four on the *fear* pictures. Some of these errors on *fear* do not appear very serious; two of the incorrect predictions were that the pictures would be judged as *fear-surprise* blends. More complex decision rules, in place of the simple majority decision rule specifying combinations of particular components in different facial areas, were also developed for over 4000 of the possible 11,000 combinations of facial components which FAST allows. These *a priori* decision rules attempted to take account of physiognomic differences, potential errors in the application of the FAST scores, and idiosyncrasies in affect display. When these more complex decision rules were applied to the FAST scores, four more photographs were correctly predicted, so that the final result was that 48 of the 51 photographs were correctly predicted.

Predictions were also made from the facial components in the three facial areas separately, and those results were consistent with Frois-Wittmann's. In most instances, the prediction made on the basis of considering components across the entire face were more correct than those made from components within a single facial area. No facial area yielded better predictions than another across all emotion categories.

Ekman and Friesen are currently conducting a study to determine whether FAST will also predict the recognition of blends, and whether it will predict the recognition of spontaneous facial behavior. The results of their first study, though limited to single posed emotions, are extremely encouraging.

SUMMARY

There have been two approaches to the study of how components of facial behavior might be related to observers' judgments of emotion. The first and most popular type of study has been to attempt to infer the location of facial components by determining whether judgments of emotion can be made from a view of one or another portion of the face. There have been no consistent results with this approach, perhaps because of methodological mistakes which are remedial, (e.g., too few stimulus persons, oversimplified division of the face into just two areas), perhaps because of flaws central to the design itself.

If stimuli judged as the same emotion sometimes show components in one facial area, sometimes in another, and sometimes across all facial areas, then this approach would yield confusing results.

The few studies which have followed the other approach, of measuring facial components and relating these to observers' judgments of emotion made from a view of the full face, have made more progress. A system for scoring facial components has succeeded in predicting how observers will judge emotion for six emotion categories, regardless of possible psychological or physiognomic differences across a sample of 28 stimulus persons. Ekman, Friesen, and Tomkins' FAST has validity for predicting the recognition value of high-agreement, single-emotion photographs, and can be a tool for studying a number of important questions. It must first be determined whether FAST can predict stimuli judged to be blends and emotions recognized from spontaneous facial behavior, and how many of the permutations of facial components contained in their scoring system are actually necessary to predict observers' judgments of emotion.

CHAPTER XVIII

What Is the Relative Contribution of Facial Behavior and Contextual Information to the Judgment of Emotion?

People rarely see a face alone without any context; when they do they usually make no inference about emotion. Usually the context includes the preceding and consequent facial behavior—the movements and position of the body, perhaps concomitant words and voice tone, the nature of the setting, what has been happening, who else is present, etc. All of these are sources of information about emotion, perhaps information which agrees with that derivable from the face alone, perhaps information discrepant from that shown in the face. The question to be addressed in this chapter is the relative contribution of context and face as sources of information. Can the face alone provide information about emotion, even though it is rare in life to see only the face? If the contextual information agrees with the facial information, is there some additive effect so that the observer is more certain about his judgment of emotion? If the two sources disagree, as, for example, if a person's face looks happy but we know he has just been told some bad news, does one source dominate or is some new more complex inference drawn which could not be made from either source alone?

Here, as in our discussion of accuracy (Chapter XV), we will present an interpretation of the literature which conflicts with that of previous reviewers (e.g., Hunt, 1941; Bruner & Tagiuri, 1954; Tagiuri, 1968). The parallel is not accidental, since their interpretation of the accuracy literature, which we disputed, was one basis for their contention that the context contributes more than, or at least always improves upon, judgments made from the face. Our disagreement with previous reviewers about the relative influence of facial and contextual information is not, however, based solely upon our different interpretation of accuracy studies, nor upon their acceptance of studies we rejected (*see* pages 50–51 for our rationale for dismissing studies using artists' sketches). More importantly, the difference is due to our having drawn a few simple conceptual distinctions which led to a reevaluation of previous experimental designs and a reinterpretation of past data. Fortunately, Frijda (1968a) also independently made some of these distinctions in a recent series of experiments and has provided evidence which agrees with our reinterpretation of past experiments (including one of his own).

Misinterpretations of the literature and the frequent use of simplistic research designs may both have been due, in part, to an underlying assumption about the face. If the face were considered to provide little, if any, information about emotion, then it would be reasonable to expect that such an impoverished source would be easily overwhelmed by any other source of information. Further, that view would not suggest the necessity to consider the *clarity* of information provided by either source, face or context. Fernberger (1928) was one of the earliest writers to reflect this view, concluding from his study of drawings of the face, "If a stimulus situation is indicated, the emotional state will be judged in accordance with that situation rather than in accordance with the facial expression." But, if the contextual information were itself ambiguous, in that observers did not know what emotion to expect (for example, "She looks at an animal in the corner of the room," a context story used in Frijda's 1958 study), and the face showed a very clear emotion, as determined independently by observer agreement, certainly the judgment of the combination would not conform to Fernberger's conclusion.

It would be possible to obtain results showing that the face was more important than the context or vice versa, depending upon whether the investigator had combined an informative face with an ambiguous context, or an ambiguous face with an informative context. All of the experiments we shall interpret have failed to recognize the necessity to consider the clarity of each source, with the sole exception of Frijda's most recent experiments, in which clarity was more of an afterthought than an integral part of the research design. We shall see, in considering data we have distinguished in terms of the clarity of each source, that Fernberger's conclusion is not always supported even when the clarity of the two sources is the same.

Bruner and Tagiuri in their review of the literature (and Tagiuri in a later review) said, "Virtually all the evidence available points to the fact that the more information about the situation in which the emotion is expressed, the more accurate and reliable are judgments of emotion" (1954, p. 636; 1968,

p. 402). Facts are rare commodities in psychology; but the data contradict this one, and their assertion ignores another necessary conceptual distinction. Not only is the clarity of the sources omitted from consideration, but Bruner and Tagiuri fail to distinguish between *concordant* and *discordant* combinations. Their conclusion is predicated on a simple additive relationship between sources, such that the combination will always be better than either source alone. While this might be true for combinations which are concordant, in that each source alone would lead to similar judgments, it is clearly not true for combinations which are discordant, in that each source alone would lead to different judgments; an additive process would simply not resolve the discrepancies. (Fernberger apparently had such discordant combinations in mind, although he failed to say so explicitly.) Even for concordant combinations, the additive hypothesis ignores the possibility that the relative weight of each source may vary with particular emotions; data we shall review show that this qualification is necessary. A last problem with the additive hypothesis, less serious than the others, is that it fails to consider the constraints due to "ceiling effects," where observers have reached near maximum agreement from one source and the addition of another could be of no measurable benefit—and, just such instances had occurred in experiments which Bruner and Tagiuri reviewed.

Bruner and Tagiuri, and Tagiuri again, made a more general criticism of research on the face and context. They wrote, "All in all, one wonders about the significance of studies of the recognition of 'facial expressions of emotions,' in isolation from context" (1954, p. 638; 1968, p. 608). Their wonder is doubt not curiosity, and obfuscates the issues. It is legitimate, we believe, to find out what kinds of information can be provided by a single source regardless of whether or not that source is typically combined with others in natural situations, and our discussions addressing the previous five questions have yielded some evidence and credible suggestion that the face, apart from knowledge of the context, can provide substantial information. The fact that the face is usually seen within a possibly informative context does not invalidate the utility of such research on the face alone; on the contrary, unless we know the contribution of each source separately, it may be impossible to untangle the complexities of the judgment process as it naturally occurs.

Contrary to Bruner and Tagiuri, we hold that understanding judgments of combined sources requires research on the information from each source alone as well as from the combination of sources, and that experiments on this problem must therefore provide three values: judgments from face alone, from context alone, and from face within context, *viz.*, the combination. This is all the more necessary since information from either source could be ambiguous or clear, matched or unequal, and could suggest the presence of the same emotion or different ones, thus allowing for concordant and discordant combinations. Those variables which are likely determinants of the judgment of the combinations cannot be specified without information about the face alone and about the context alone.

We will briefly consider what might be implied by the term *context*, and then discuss different aspects of the clarity of a source, before outlining some of the methodological problems common to the experiments we will review. Information about the context in which facial behavior occurred could encompass quite a number of different phenomena: stable characteristics of the social setting, such as the task, the physical locale, etc.; stable characteristics of the participants, such as deomographic variations and roles; and transient events which precede or follow the facial behavior, such as events involving inanimate objects, the behavior of other participants, and the facial or other behavior of the stimulus person.

Three different procedures have been utilized to provide contextual information, none of them comparable in the amount or type of information they convey or in their credibility to the observer. One technique has been to show an entire still photograph, often including more than just the behavior of the stimulus person, sometimes indicating preceding and consequent events, sometimes conveying information about stable setting and personal characteristics. Another technique has been to present a verbal description or story about the context in which the facial behavior occurred; but even here, where it is most feasible to control systematically for the type and amount of information given, this has not always been done. The third technique involves preceding the facial behavior with motion picture film sequences of other contextual events.

Regardless of the technique they employ, investigators should either systematically vary some of the types of contextual information in order to study them, or, at least, maintain some constancy in the type and amount of contextual information provided across their experimental conditions, so it is possible to reach some determination from their data, no matter how limited their sampling of types of contextual information. Unfortunately, neither has been done; type and amount of contextual information furnished over trials within almost all experiments have varied unsystematically.

The phrase *source clarity* refers to differences in the amount or type of information about emotion available to observers when they are exposed to a single source—face or context. There are at least three aspects of source clarity: ambiguity, message complexity, and strength. The *ambiguity* of a source could be measured by the extent of agreement among observers about the presence or likelihood of a single emotion in terms of category judgments, or the variance in their judgments if an emotion dimension task is used. Some faces, for example, will yield agreement among almost all observers; other faces will yield agreement among perhaps half of the observers, with the rest either opting for a second emotion (shortly we will consider such bimodal distributions which imply blends) or randomly distributing their choices; and some stimuli will be essentially ambiguous, eliciting no agreement among observers. In a parallel fashion, some stimuli will elicit a very small variance on an emotion scale such as pleasant-unpleasant, others a moderate variance, and still others a sufficiently large variance to suggest that the stimulus is ambiguous.[34]

The *message complexity* of a source could be measured by whether a single emotion or a blend of emotions is observed, the former being considered less complex than the latter. Determination of a blend is better made from a judgment task which allows observers to record their impression about the presence of two or more emotions (e.g., Nummenmaa, pages 123–124) than inferred from a bimodal distribution when only one judgment is allowed.[35] We have called a blend less clear than a single emotion stimulus because the presence of a blend might allow for a greater variety of interpretations, more potential for shifting away from the judgment of a single source when the combined sources are observed—but this is, of course, an empirical question which has not been studied.

The *strength* of a source could be measured by intensity of the emotion observed, disregarding or holding constant the judgment about the nature of the emotion. Two contexts might both be associated with anger, or yield the same mean on a pleasant-unpleasant scale, but one context might yield low intensity judgments, while the other might yield high intensity judgments.

---

[34] There is a problem with bipolar scale judgments about what the midpoint of the scale represents. A barely pleasant, or a barely unpleasant, stimulus might appropriately be rated at the midpoint, either because the judges could not attribute any emotion to it or because a random distribution of judgments would produce a midpoint mean. But the variance may be no different for stimuli having a midpoint mean, even if that midpoint provides information for one stimulus (barely pleasant) and indicates inappropriateness for another (agreement in the use of the midpoint because the scale is not relevant to the stimulus).

[35] The problem with inferring a blend from a bimodal distribution of judgments on a task which allowed only a single choice is that this distribution may not always indicate that most observers really saw both emotions, and simply chose one or the other; alternately, it can as well indicate divergent, nonoverlapping judgments by the two groups of observers (*see* Chapter V).

All three aspects of source clarity need to be considered, for they are interrelated. Intensity of a source is relevant to each message if the source involves a blend; agreement may vary about intensity judgments, and thus there may be more or less ambiguity about the intensity of a source. It would be preferable in planning experiments on the face and context to utilize all three measures of source clarity, but no experiment has determined the relative clarity of its sources on more than one index. Even more problematical, no experiment has systematically manipulated clarity (even if measured only one way) pairing high, moderate, and low clarity stimuli from each source. Unwittingly, however, some of these combinations have occurred, and the investigator has drawn unwarranted conclusions in that he did not consider that his results were limited to the particular clarity combinations he happened upon. Even when clarity of sources is not to be an independent variable systematically explored, information about the clarity of each source must be provided in order to determine whether the sources were evenly or unevenly matched. And information about the clarity of each source will also reveal whether concordant or discordant combinations have been studied. Some of the studies we will examine did not specify which type of combination they were investigating.

In addition, these experiments share some previously described methodological flaws with the experiments which addressed the first five substantive questions. Here, too, it is important to sample a number of different emotions for each source. Only one investigator did that (Frijda, 1968a), and he considered only two emotion dimensions; but since he found some differences in the relative influence of the face and context as a function of the emotion sampled, we must regard with considerable caution generalizations drawn from experiments which do not specify the relevant emotions. Again, it is important to have a reasonable sampling of stimulus persons whose facial behavior makes up one of the sources and, in addition, to have a representative sampling of contexts. Most studies have used the facial behavior of only one person, usually an actor posing.

The reader might well wonder at this point why with all these defects we bother to discuss any of the experiments. There are three reasons. The first is to convince the reader that the conclusions of past reviewers are not only unwarranted, in that they fail to specify the relevant parameters of the phenomena, but unfounded, in that what data there are suggest just the reverse of what has been concluded. The second is to illustrate the methodological requirements for research on this topic by applying them to the interpretation of past data. And the third is to report the few findings which hint at what future research may show.

Goldberg (1951) performed the only experiment in which the context was defined by the preceding motion picture film sequences. Observers watched two different versions of a motion picture film containing four scenes. In both films, the fourth scene—a woman screaming—was the same, and the observers judged the emotion shown in that scene by choosing an emotion word from a list. In both film versions, the first scene was also the same—a child riding a tricycle—but in one version the two intervening scenes suggested an automobile accident, while in the other they suggested amiable play between the child and a man. Goldberg showed both versions to two groups of observers, varying the film seen first.

We believe that the data which are most relevant to measuring the influence of the differing context (previous film episodes, accident, or play) on the judgment of the scream are only the observations from each group for the first film they viewed. After seeing either version, the second film might well be rated quite differently simply because the subjects had figured out the experimenter's hypothesis. Goldberg did report that there was a significant order-effect for the judgments of the accident film; it was judged as more fearful when seen first. In analyzing Goldberg's published data, we found that there was also an order-effect for the play film; it was judged as less fearful and more joyful when seen second. The presence of this order-effect does suggest that the most conservative test of Goldberg's hypothesis about context would be from the first judgments of each group of observers where there is no question of their being contaminated by previous film watching.

In comparing the judgments of the accident versus the play context on the judgments of the scream scene, Goldberg had calculated chi-squares over all conditions, and also within each group of observers, and found significant differences. Even when our precaution is employed, and only the first observations in each group are compared, a significant chi-square shows that the context had an influence, but the influence is not nearly as dramatic.

Goldberg concluded from his findings that "the concept formed by the perception of a motion picture film is not dependent upon the reaction to the individual scenes that have been cut and spliced together, but rather on the sequence as a whole" (1951, p. 71). We question this interpretation for a number of reasons. Its generality is in doubt since only one stimulus person and only one facial stimulus were studied and, further, there is no information provided about the interpretation of the separate scenes to which Goldberg's conclusion refers. Perhaps more importantly, while there was a significant shift in the judgment of some observers (24% more observers judged the scream in the play version as anger or joy than in the accident version, and 21% fewer observers judged the scream in the play version as fear than in the accident version), Goldberg overlooked what his data showed in terms of the stability of judgment of the scream regardless of the preceding context. Seventy-seven percent of the observers still called the scream in the play version fear, as compared to 98% in the accident version. Although no conclusion is possible from this study because of limited sampling of emotions and stimulus persons, and the lack of data on each source, the results can be used to support either the Fernberger hypothesis about contextual dominance, or just the reverse, depending upon which aspect of the data is emphasized. The preceding context influenced the judgment of the face for about a fourth of the sample of observers while better than 70% of the observers judged the face as showing the same emotion regardless of differences in preceding context.

Munn's study is probably the best known work on the influence of the context on judgments of the face, and is most frequently cited in support of the view that contextual information is the *sine qua non* for judgments of emotion from the face or, at the least, will always improve judgments of the face alone. Munn utilized candid camera photographs of presumably emotional situations as his stimuli; to provide contextual information he showed the full photograph including everything captured by the original photographer. Judgments made from that source were compared with judgments made from the same photographs cropped to show the face alone.

There are a number of problems in Munn's experiment. First, there are no judgments from the contextual source independent of the facial information; thus there is no way of assessing what information came from just the context, and what information from just the face. We have tried to remedy this defect by substituting judgment data we collected by giving Munn's verbal descriptions of each context to a group of observers and asking them to choose a single emotion from a list of six categories, and an option of no-emotion (*see* pages 91–93 for a description of this study and the use of these data to establish an accuracy criterion). It would have been preferable if Munn had obscured the face from the whole photographs and shown those stimuli to observers to determine the information available from his contexts; but since we did not have his stimuli, we were unable to attempt that.

A second problem relates to the use of Munn's procedure for presenting contextual information. Granting that contexts defined by cameramen may be more believable to the observer than a verbal story of a supposed context, nevertheless it is difficult to obtain comparable contexts, similar in the type and amount of information they furnish. That is, one such photograph may show the emotional reactions of other participants, another may show the event which elicited the reaction, etc. If such a procedure is to be used, then there should be some systematic sampling of different photographs balanced in terms of the type and amount of information they provide. A third problem is that Munn did not consider whether he was studying discordant or concordant source combinations, and while most of his data are relevant only to the latter, there are two discordant combinations as well. A fourth problem is his failure to consider source clarity for either face or context; examination of his data and the auxiliary data we collected shows that for all but one item there is similar clarity for each source, and for some stimuli the clarity was moderate, so there was room for improvement in judgment.

One interesting virtue of Munn's procedure is that it does furnish an opportunity to assess the relative value of each source. Since these are actual photographs of actual events rather than the contrived contexts used by Goldberg and in most of the other studies we will consider, a comparison of the clarity of each source—face and context provides some impression as to which source yields more information. This comparison is limited, however, by the small number of stimuli and of stimulus persons, the unknown nature of the principle of selection of stimuli by first the cameraman and then Munn, and by our reliance on observers' judgments of verbal descriptions of the context to measure that source, which may under- or overestimate what observers might have said if they saw the actual photograph of the situation without the face.

In reanalyzing Munn's data, we have disregarded the results from 5 of his 14 stimuli, all of which were athletic events and were judged by our observers as typically not associated with any one emotion. For the remaining stimuli, we have reorganized judgments into the emotion categories suggested earlier in Table 2.

Seven of the nine stimuli listed in Table 11 involved concordant combinations, where each source judged separately yielded similar results. These have been further divided on the basis of high and moderate clarity of both sources. The data permit two tests of Bruner and Tagiuri's additive hypothesis. First, the column labeled "Combination Judgment Minus the Judgment of the Highest Single Source," shows that there was *no* consistent pattern to suggest that the combination of face and context is always better than the source which is superior when observed alone. Second, if we compare the combination judgment with the face-alone judgment, again there is no strong trend; for three items there was no difference, for one item the face alone yielded higher agreement than the combination of face and context, and for three items the combination was better than face alone. So the additive hypothesis, that the combination of sources will always be better than either source alone, is not supported, nor is the more limited hypothesis that the combination of face and context is better than the face alone.

TABLE 11

Reanalysis of Munn's Data on the Face and Context

Type of Combination	Verbal Description of Situation Given to Observers (N=35)	Judgment of Verbal Description	Judgment of Face Alone	Combination: Judgment of Face Plus Picture	Combination Judgment Minus Highest Single Source
Concordant High Clarity for Each Source	1. Girl Running into Ocean	91% Happy	97% Happy	97% Happy	0
	2. Jitterbug Clapping Hands to Music	97% Happy	86% Happy	92% Happy	−5
	3. Girl Running from Ghost	94% Fear	94% Fear	88% Fear	−6
Concordant Moderate Clarity for Each Source	4. Girl Photographed over Transom while Dressing	56% Surprise	66% Surprise	72% Surprise	+6
	5. Man Holding Hand of Drowned Person	63% Sad	74% Sad	74% Sad	0
	6. Porter Leading Burned Man from Scene of Airplane Crash	56% Fear	41% Fear*	45% Fear	−11
	7. Man with Hand Stretched towards Hostile Crowd	65% Fear 65% Sad	63% Fear Sad	74% Fear Sad	+9
Discordant Low Clarity for Each Source	8. Girl Photographed over Transom while in Bath	44% Anger 38% Surprise	26% Surprise 28% Fear	75% Surprise	Interpretation more Influenced by Face than Context
Discordant Moderate Clarity for One Source, Ambiguous for the Other	9. Man Who Is Holding Strikebreaker by the Coat Collar	68% Anger	8% Anger	78% Anger	Interpretation Influenced by Context

* We credited Anxiety as well as Fear as a Fear Category Response.

Table 11 also allows a test of the question of which source—face or context, usually provides more information. There seems to be no general trend, but a variation with the item. The face judgments were higher than the context judgments for three of the items, the context higher than the face for four items, and no difference was found on the remaining two items. Fernberger's hypothesis, that the context always dominates the face, involves essentially the same question, but can be evaluated only for discordant combinations, of which there were only two. In the one instance where there was similar clarity for both sources (#8) the combination judgment agreed more with the facial judgment than with the contextual. The last item does not provide a relevant case because the face was judged to be ambiguous and the context informative, and the combination was judged as the same as the nonambiguous source.

To summarize briefly our evaluation of Munn's experiment, his design can be criticized on a number of grounds. The limited sampling of faces, emotions, and contexts prevents any conclusions, but what data there were support neither Fernberger's context dominance hypothesis nor Bruner and Tagiuri's additive hypothesis.

Vinacke (1949) performed an experiment similar to Munn's, also using candid photographs, and showing one group of observers only the face, the other group the entire photograph including the face. His verbal descriptions of the contexts shown in his 20 photographs were judged by our group of observers; only six were judged by the majority as probably being associated with a single emotion. We will not report the results on these six photographs, since the results are comparable to those we have given for Munn, and they are open to the same criticisms.

Goodenough and Tinker (1931) performed the first experiment on context to employ story descriptions of the context. Their study is notable because it is the only one before 1969 to include data on the clarity of each source in addition to judgments of the combinations. It is hard to understand why their findings have received so little attention and, further, why later researchers, some of whom do cite that study, did not profit from their research design. While their substantive results are limited because of the use of just a few stimuli of just one stimulus person, that is so for every study we can report, even Frijda's most recent experiments. Goodenough and Tinker did not consider differentiating among stimuli in terms of the amount of clarity in each source, but neither has anyone else, and they deserve praise for at least measuring the clarity of each source separately.

Goodenough and Tinker selected four of Feleky's (1914) posed photographs intended to represent four emotions—fear, anger, disgust, and sympathy. The judgments of their observers of only the faces rated two stimuli as high clarity (96% agreement for the fear and disgust pictures), and two as moderate clarity (sympathy judged as such by 75% of the observers, and the intended anger picture judged as fear by 78% of the observers; we will treat that picture as showing fear, not anger, since that is how it was judged). The four stories intended to connote these same four emotions were all high clarity, 100% of the observers having judged each story to represent the emotion intended by the authors.

TABLE 12

Reanalysis of Goodenough & Tinker's Data on Face and Context

			Emotion Judgments of Observers Who Received Both Face and Context (Percentages)			
				Context		
			Disgust	Fear	Sympathy	Anger
A. Discordant High Clarity for Each Source	Face	Disgust	—	43 Disgust 41 Fear	47 Disgust 46 Sympathy	69 Disgust
		Fear	49 Disgust 42 Fear		50 Fear 47 Sympathy	78 Fear
B. Discordant and Concordant Higher Clarity for Context than Face	Face Moderate Clarity			Context—High Clarity		
		Fear	72 Disgust	96 Fear	43 Sympathy	No Data
		Sympathy	69 Disgust	87 Fear	—	74 Anger

Table 12 shows the two types of source combinations furnished by this experiment. The top part of the table shows the results for the judgments of discordant combinations in which the clarity of the two sources is comparable. These data do not support Fernberger's conclusion. There is no combination which fits the context-dominance expectation. Instead, in two of the combinations, the face dominates the context: disgust face dominates anger context, fear face dominates an anger context. No conclusion can be drawn, however, about facial dominance, without replication with other stories for the anger context and other stimuli for the fear and disgust faces.

The second part of the table shows combination judgments of stimuli in which the context had greater clarity (higher agreement among observers) than the face. In each instance, the combination is dominated by the context. Again conclusions are difficult because of the limited sampling of either source, but it seems reasonable to expect that with discordant combinations in which source clarity differs, the clearer source will dominate. If the face had been clearer than the context, then for these same emotions the face might well have dominated the combination judgments.

In sum, Goodenough and Tinker's experiment does not provide the basis for any conclusions, because of limitations in the sampling of both faces and contexts, but it is exemplary in terms of providing data on each source alone. Their findings do, however, raise serious doubt about the validity of the general assertion that one of these sources (the context) will always have more influence than the other (face), when the two sources are of comparable clarity, and the combination of the two is discordant. Frijda's most recent experiments, to be interpreted next, essentially replicate Goodenough and Tinker's findings.

Frijda (1968a), in a series of experiments, followed much the same design as Goodenough and Tinker.[36] The major limitation of these experiments, as with the Goodenough and Tinker study, is the limited sampling of stimulus persons (only one), of faces of that person (four in one study, and three pictures in each of the other two studies), and of context stories (6, 9, and 9).

In all three experiments, this procedure was followed. First, photographs were rated by the observers on ten 7-point bipolar scales; next, situation descriptions were rated by these same observers on the same bipolar scales; a week later, the combinations of photographs and contexts were judged by these same observers on these same scales. In the first experiment, no systematic sampling procedures were followed in the selection of the four photographs. When the ratings on the discordant combinations were analyzed by comparing the judgments across all 10 scales for each source separately, Frijda found that the face dominated, in that the shift away from the context-only rating was twice as great as the shift away from the face-only rating. The second and third experiments were planned to explore this matter by systematically selecting stimuli for both sources in terms of an emotion dimension.

In the second study, three faces were employed—one judged as pleasant, one judged as unpleasant, and one expected to be judged in the middle of the

---

[36] We have not discussed the Frijda and Philipszoon (1963) study, since it did not provide information about each source, its methodology has been criticized by Rump (1960), and its quite ambiguous findings have been far improved upon by Frijda's recent experiments which solved some of the earlier methodological problems.

scale, or neutral, but actually judged as slightly unpleasant. There were nine situation descriptions—four unpleasant and five pleasant. Frijda does not report his data in a way which allows examination of whether there was differing clarity for the stimuli in each source (as indicated by the variance) and if this affected the results. For all discordant combinations, however, he noted that again the face dominated the context; the correlation between face-only and combination ratings was 0.67, while that between context-only and combination ratings was −0.49. "To judge from these data," Frijda wrote, "if someone behaves (face) happily, or sad, when circumstances (context) make us expect otherwise, we rather believe his behavior than our expectations" (1968a, p. 45). In the concordant combinations there was a nonsignificant trend for the context to dominate, but Frijda attributes this to the greater polarity (perhaps indicating higher clarity) for contexts as compared to faces.

The third experiment was similar to the second except that the selection principle was in terms of his dimension of active versus passive attending. Three pictures representing each pole and a midpoint, and nine stories about context varying on this dimension, were used. For all discordant combinations the face again dominated the context; the correlation between face-only and combination ratings was 0.87, while the correlation between context-only and combination ratings was −0.36. And, again, there was no significant tendency for the context to dominate in the concordant combinations or for the agreement, as measured by the variances, to be less for combinations than for the separate sources.

Frijda attempted to determine whether the clarity of the face (variance) might be related to the extent to which judgments of the combination shifted away from the face to the context judgment. He found such a relationship in the second experiment but not in the first. Frijda also examined whether the shifts in judgment differed in relation to the particular emotions involved in each source. He found a greater shift away from the face (context had more influence) for the happy face when it was paired with a sad story than for a sad picture when it was paired with a happy story; there was more shift away from the face for the passive picture paired with an active context than for an active face paired with a passive context.

In attempting to explain these findings, Frijda examined the observers' descriptions of how they resolved discrepant information and suggested the operation of four different cognitive mechanisms, but these are the weakest data in his experiment. One of Frijda's four cognitive mechanisms implies what we earlier discussed in terms of display rules and masking of emotion (Chapter IV). The concept of display rules and our earlier interpretation of why subjects smiled so often in Landis' experiment (page 81) would suggest that the difference between the sad and happy face might be attributed to the observers interpreting smiles which are discrepant from context to be a mask, but there should be no similar expectation about sad faces acting as a mask of happy feelings. The difference between the passive and active faces might be due to the former having less distinctive facial components than the latter, and, thus, in that sense being more ambiguous; or it might be that a passive face is more frequently a mask than is an active face. These interpretations cannot be actually tested from Frijda's data, although some of his evidence supports them.

Frijda's experiments disconfirm both the additive hypothesis and the context dominance hypothesis. They further suggest the necessity to consider particular emotions in each source and the value of including measures of the cognitive operations employed by the observers to resolve discrepant information in discordant combinations. Conclusions are not possible, primarily because of the limited sampling of emotions and stimulus persons, but Frijda's study certainly points to the fruitfulness of research on this problem.

There is another potential problem in the design employed by Frijda and by Goodenough and Tinker. Conceivably, when the context information is provided through a verbal story and that information is discordant with the information from a facial photograph, the facial source will dominate because the observers view the photograph as a more direct representation and, thus, as more believable than a verbal story. This is not to suggest that actions must always speak louder than words, but that within an experiment the two sources may differ in credibility by virtue of the medium of their presentation. If that is so, such findings could misrepresent what may actually occur in natural settings, where the contextual information would be just as credible as the facial information. The use of one medium, e.g., photographs or films, to provide both the contextual information and the facial information might circumvent this *potential* problem.

SUMMARY

No conclusions can be drawn about the relative influence of information from facial behavior and information about the context in judgments of emotion when both are known by the observer. The only exception is that the context dominance hypothesis of Fernberger and the additive hypothesis of

Bruner and Tagiuri have been shown to be unsupported by what data are available. There seems to be no question that either source, face or context, can on given occasions be more salient or more useful or more of a determinant of the combined judgment than the other. But this statement is surely insufficient and only points to the necessity for research on three questions.

First, what are the parameters of both sources which determine their relative influence on the judgment of the combinations? We have argued that the parameters must include the clarity of each source, preferably measured in regards to ambiguity, message complexity, and strength; the distinct emotions associated with each source; and the pairing of sources to yield discordant and concordant combinations. Thus moderate clarity, happy faces could be paired with moderate clarity, happy contexts; with high clarity, happy contexts; with moderate clarity, fearful contexts; with extreme clarity, fearful contexts; etc. Further, there must be representative sampling of stimulus persons and facial behaviors for each of these possibilities, and different context definitions in terms of the type and amount of contextual information, since high clarity contextual sources may still differ in the type of information provided, and this difference might be relevant to whether the context dominates the face or not, or to the type of cognitive mechanism employed to resolve the discrepancy.

The second research problem is the specification of the particular cognitive mechanisms employed to resolve discrepant information between the face and the context. Frijda has made a beginning on this problem, and we have suggested above only some of the parameters of the sources which should be considered in research on the cognitive mechanisms for resolving discordant combinations.

A third research problem is to investigate the nature of those occasions when the face provides more information than the context, when the context provides more information than the face, and when each provides influential information, and the resolution of the discrepancy involves a reinterpretation of both sources. The answer may lie in part with individual or cultural differences; some people or peoples may generally provide trustworthy facial behavior, others may be notorious for deceptive facial behavior. The answer may lie in part also in the nature of the social setting in which the facial behavior occurs. Ekman and Friesen (1969a) have specified some of the parameters of social interactions where the face is a less reliable source of information than the context, although they did not consider the converse, the nature of the social interactions where facial behavior is trustworthy, perhaps more so than social context. Goffman (1963) has offered some notions about the nature of conversational behavior which might provide leads for specifying the particular points within a conversation when either face or context might be more useful.[37]

---

[37] Our discussion of the face and context may seem to contradict the role assigned to cognition in Schacter's theory of emotion (Schacter & Singer, 1962). But Schacter was concerned with how we know our own emotions, not how we judge the emotions of others, and he considered two sources of information (physiological changes and context) but did not consider facial behavior. We will consider how findings on the face and emotion pertain to theories of emotion in Chapter XX.

CHAPTER XIX

What Are the Similarities and Differences in Facial Behavior across Cultures?

There has been a long, heated controversy over the question of universals in the face and emotion. Those who argue that there are universal facial expressions of emotion hypothesize that the relationship between specific facial behaviors and particular emotions is innate, or is the result of certain learning experiences which are common to all men regardless of culture. Those who argue that there are no universals claim that the relationship between particular facial behaviors and particular emotions is learned in a fashion which varies with each culture or subculture. The dispute has been based largely on anecdote and unsystematized observation. The culture-specific view has been predominant, marshalling wide acceptance within psychology and anthropology. Very recently, however, it has been challenged, particularly by the ethologists, but again without much data. In the last few years, a consistent body of evidence has accumulated which conclusively demonstrates that there *is* a pan-cultural element in the association of facial behavior with emotion.

   Darwin (1872) proposed that there are universal facial behaviors for each emotion and, in supporting this claim, was the first to utilize a judgment procedure in the study of facial behavior; but no quantitative research was done on this topic until 1941. LaBarre's (1947, 1962) and Birdwhistell's (1963) writings on cultural differences in emotion received wide attention and were generally interpreted as evidence that the facial behaviors associated with emotions were socially learned and culturally variable. However, they had not systematically gathered quantitative data, but had relied upon anecdotal impressions, the descriptions of novelists, or anthropological reports.

Klineberg has recently said that the axiom, "what shows on the face is written there by culture," is an unfair view of his work (Izard, 1969, p. 18). In his original writing, he anticipated some of our discussion of display rules (Chapter IV) in proposing that there are three ways in which social determinants can influence emotional behavior: by determining which situations evoke which emotions, by conditioning the amount of overt emotional behavior which is culturally acceptable in a situation, and by directing the manner in which the emotions manifest themselves. In regard to the last, he wrote, "There are undoubtedly certain types of expressive behavior which are common to all human societies," (1940, p. 176) probably the manifestations of happiness, fear, and sadness.

LaBarre took the opposite view; i.e., ". . . there is no 'natural' language of emotional gesture" (1947, p. 55); but the statement itself emphasizes his failure to distinguish gesture from facial behavior associated with an emotion. Birdwhistell shares LaBarre's view, although he did distinguish gestures from facial behaviors associated with emotion: "When I first became interested in studying body motion . . . I anticipated a research strategy which could first isolate universal signs of feeling that were species specific. . . . As research proceeded, and even before the development of kinesics, it became clear that this search for universals was culture bound. . . . there are probably no universal symbols of emotional state. . . ." (1963, p. 126).

Arguing just the opposite view, but admittedly without direct evidence to support their claim, F. Allport (1924), Asch (1952), and Tomkins (1962, 1963) have provided different theoretical bases for hypothesizing invariants in facial behavior related to emotion, regardless of culture. These researchers also recognized there would be cultural differences in facial behavior as well, and each made a partial attempt to explain these cultural variations in facial behavior.

Thus there has been considerable controversy over the question of whether there are any pan-cultural aspects to facial behavior associated with emotion, any invariants in the relationship between facial behavior and specific emotions, but neither side in the argument has had systematically gathered quantitative data to support their view.

This is one question on which the data are now quite clear. Eight experiments have been conducted on facial behavior in different cultures and all have provided evidence of universals. Six studies, utilizing a judgment procedure, have shown that the same facial behavior are associated with the same emotions by observers from different cultures. One study has shown that emotions posed by members of a preliterate culture are accurately judged by members of a literate culture. The eighth experiment used a components rather than a judgment approach, directly measuring facial behavior in the same eliciting circumstance in two cultures. The data from the first two studies are somewhat confused, largely because of limitations in the sampling of facial stimuli. The other six studies, however, unfold a very consistent picture.

Triandis and Lambert (1958) compared urban Greek, rural Greek, and urban U.S. observers in their judgments of the facial behavior of Schlosberg's set of posed photographs (Engen, Levy, & Schlosberg, 1957). They found evidence of similarities and differences. By and large the stimuli received the same ratings on Schlosberg's three dimensions of emotion across the three groups of observers. There were significant intercorrelations between the judgments of U.S. and Greek urban, U.S. and Greek rural, and the Greek urban and rural observers on the Pleasantness dimension, (0.91, 0.82, and 0.86), on the Attention-Rejection dimension, (0.82, 0.88, 0.83), and on the Sleep-Tension dimension, (0.76, 0.67, 0.66).

There was a cultural difference in the relationships among the judgments on the three dimensions. The Greeks rated pictures they judged as *unpleasant* more towards *attention* and *tension*, while the U.S. observers did the same for pictures they judged as *pleasant*. The authors mentioned that interpretation of this difference was difficult, but suggested that the U.S. observers were more activist and instrumentally-oriented about emotion than the Greek observers.

Another difference in dimension judgments among observer groups was between the two urban groups (U.S. and Greek) and the rural sample. On all three dimensions, the mean rating on the pictures was more similar between the urban groups than between either and the rural sample. Triandis and Lambert thought this might be due to stereotyping of judgments on the basis of having seen commercial motion pictures; but it could just as well have been due to the different types of judgment tasks used with the rural sample.

Another cultural difference was found in the judgments based on Woodworth's six emotion categories. There were more random judgments among the Greek observers on this task than on the dimension judgments. This finding led Osgood (1966) to conclude that the affective meanings (dimension judgments) of facial expression are more stable across languages and cultures than the referential or denotative meanings (category judgments). But, subsequent research by others has found consistent category judgments across a great number of cultures and language groups. This particular finding of Triandis and Lambert may be due, as Izard said (1969), to peculiarities of the

Lightfoot series of photographs which Schlosberg had posed specifically to represent differences on his dimensions.

In sum, the Triandis and Lambert study found evidence for both similarities and differences between the groups of observers they compared, but for two reasons it is difficult to untangle what accounted for either the similarities or the differences. The data are limited to judgments of only one stimulus person; and, there was no control for the amount of visual contact among the groups of observers.

Vinacke expected to find differences among his groups of Caucasian, Japanese, and Chinese observers (all from Hawaii) in their judgments of Caucasian (1949) and of Oriental faces (Vinacke & Fong, 1955). The 21 Caucasian stimuli and 28 Oriental stimuli were photographs from magazines, selected by Munn's technique as showing presumably emotional behavior. The three groups of observers differed significantly only in the extent of their agreement about a particular emotion; but there was a slight tendency for the observers to reach higher agreement in judging their own than the other group's behavior. Vinacke concluded that this could be "linked with nation-racial ancestry," but admitted his evidence was weak. He did not, however, have the same set of observers judge both Caucasian and Oriental stimuli, and the slight differences he did obtain may well have been due to the sampling of observers in his two experiments.

Vinacke recognized the necessity to achieve visual isolation among his groups of observers, and explained his failure to show significant cultural differences as possibly due to his use of groups from Hawaii, all of whom had extensive mutual contact. Another problem with Vinacke's experiments is the questionable relevance of his stimuli to emotion; we have only investigated his information about the contexts in which the Caucasian faces occurred, but that did show that only 6 out of his 20 situations were judged by observers as having relevance to emotion (*see* Chapter XV). Agreement among all of his groups of observers was usually low, but, in any case, despite his attempt to find evidence of cultural differences, he obtained just the opposite.

Dickey and Knower (1941) conducted the first experiment comparing groups of observers from different cultures in their judgments of the same set of facial behaviors. Junior and Senior high school boys and girls in the U.S. and Mexico City judged 22 photographs of posed emotions, choosing among emotion categories. In both cultures, the same facial behaviors were judged as showing the same emotion, although agreement was consistently higher among the Mexican than among the U.S. observers. Dickey and Knower interpreted this difference in extent of agreement as due to the greater sensitivity of Mexicans to the communicative symbols of action. It is difficult

TABLE 13

Literate Cultures, Percentage that Same Emotion Is Identified with Same Stimulus within Each Group

	Dickey & Knower		Izard									Ekman & Friesen				
	Mexican	U.S.	U.S.	English	German	Swedish	French	Swiss	Greek	African	Japanese	Japanese	Brazil	Chile	Argentina	U.S.
Happy	97	95	97	96	98	96	94	97	93	68	94	87	97	90	94	97
Fear	71	55	76	67	84	89	83	67	68	48	58	71	77	78	68	88
Surprise	54	43	90	80	85	80	84	85	80	49	79	87	82	88	93	91
Anger	86	69	69	81	83	82	91	92	80	51	57	63	82	76	72	69
Disgust/Contempt	61	47	82	84	73	88	78	78	87	55	56	82	86	85	79	82
Sad	61	51	73	74	67	71	70	70	54	32	67	74	82	90	85	73
Number of Observers	616	1244	89	62	158	41	67	36	50	29	60	29	40	119	168	99
Number of Categories Other Than These Listed Here	5	5	2	2	2	2	2	2	2	2	2	0	0	0	0	0

157

to know what their difference in agreement means; it was not replicated, and Izard's work and Ekman's have not revealed any similar superiority of other cultural groups over U.S. observers.

In any case, they did find that the faces were judged as showing the same emotion in the two cultures; however, the evidence for cross-cultural similarity is limited by their observers' lack of visual isolation and by the smallness of their sample of stimulus persons (only two). Their results (all age groups and sexes combined) are reported in Table 13, with the data reorganized so that it could be presented for the six categories of emotion we have been considering. The table is organized so that one may examine any row, or set of photographs assumed to represent a particular emotion, and compare the percentage of each group which identified those stimuli as showing the expected emotion. The particular stimuli used to represent each emotion, of course, will differ for the three investigators listed in the table.

Izard (1969) developed his own set of 32 photographs, selected on the basis of agreement among pilot groups of observers. These were presented to observers in eight different language culture groups, who made judgments using emotion category labels which had been translated into their own language. The results, shown in Table 13, were quite consistent across cultures; (we have not included the results on *shame* and *interest*).

Izard's weakest results (while still greater than chance in terms of cross-cultural agreement) were from his Africans and Japanese. The Africans were persons from different parts of Africa living in France, and Izard believed there may have been translation problems. The Japanese results may well have been lowered by translation difficulties; Ekman obtained better agreement with his Japanese sample, and his translators were critical of the particular emotion translations used by Izard.

The only major limit on Izard's findings of cross-cultural similarity in the judgment of emotion from facial behavior is the lack of visual isolation among any of the groups of observers compared, a point we will look into shortly.

Ekman and Friesen, in collaboration with Tomkins, selected stimuli which appeared free of the influence of any display rules to control or mask emotion, and which showed the facial components they hypothesized to be specific to each emotion. They were developing at that time their procedure for systematically scoring from photographs or films the facial components associated with emotion; *see* Facial Affect Scoring Technique (FAST), Chapter XVI. When pictures had to be selected for the cross-cultural study, FAST was not completed, and they could not select stimuli on the basis of FAST scores. Instead, they applied FAST's specifications informally as they examined and selected pictures. Thirty photographs of 14 different stimulus persons met their criteria, including pictures from Ekman and Friesen's (1968) study of mental patients, and from the studies of Frois-Wittmann (1930), Schlosberg (Engen, Levy, & Schlosberg, 1957), and Tomkins (1964). These photographs were shown to observers in five literate cultures who chose an emotion category from a list of six translated into their own language. These results, shown in Table 13, again reveal that in literate cultures the same facial stimuli are judged as indicating the same emotions regardless of the culture of the observer.

But these results, like the results of Dickey and Knower; Izard; Triandis and Lambert; and Vinacke, could be regarded as not necessarily persuasive for the view that there are pan-cultural elements in facial behavior. Instead, these data could be interpreted as evidence that culturally variable learning is the sole basis for the association of facial behaviors with emotions. On the ground that there was some shared visual input among the cultures compared, it could be argued that everyone had learned to recognize the same set of conventions, or at least had become familiar with each other's different facial behavior through this shared visual source. This argument could be met by showing that members of a visually isolated culture recognize the same emotions for the same stimuli as do members of literate cultures.

Ekman, Sorenson, and Friesen (1969) conducted studies on the recognition of emotion in two preliterate cultures, Borneo and New Guinea. They used the same stimuli for which positive results had been obtained in five literate cultures. They encountered difficulty in utilizing the usual judgment task, in which the observer is shown a photograph and asked to choose an emotion label from a list of emotions. They have published only their data on the observers in these two preliterate cultures who had had most contact with Westerners. While those results were similar to the results from literate cultures, the data were weaker, and the pan-cultural theory was still open to argument, inasmuch as those observers were not visually isolated.

In a second study, Ekman and Friesen (1971) had better success, utilizing a judgment task first described by Dashiell (1927) for working with young children. The observer was given three photographs at once, each showing a face, and was told a story which involved only one emotion; the observer then pointed to the face he deemed appropriate to the story. Figure 2 shows a set of three photographs and one of the stories used in this study. The observers were from the Fore language group in New Guinea. The following criteria were established to minimize visual contact with Western cultures: they had seen no movies or magazines; they neither spoke nor understood English or Pidgin; they had not lived in any of the Western settlements or government

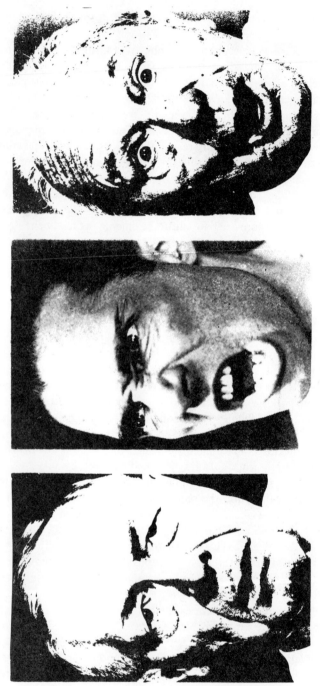

Fig. 2. These are examples of the photograph sets utilized in the study of emotion recognition among preliterate observers in New Guinea.

The photograph on the left, one of Tomkins' stimuli, has been judged as sadness across literate cultures. The picture in the middle, one of Frois-Wittmann's stimuli, has been judged as anger within literate cultures. The photograph on the right, one of Tomkins' stimuli, has been judged as surprise within literate cultures.

In the experiment conducted in New Guinea with observers from a preliterate culture, all three photographs were shown at once, and a translator asked the observer to pick the face that would occur if "this child died and he felt sad." 79% of the 189 adult observers in New Guinea selected the picture on the left as fitting that story. This confirms that the same facial behaviour is selected for the same emotion concept in this more visually isolated preliterate culture.

TABLE 14

Identification of Emotion Photographs by Visually Isolated Preliterate Observers (Ekman & Friesen)

Emotion Category Described in the Story	Percent Choice of the Emotion Expected in Terms of Agreement With the Judgments of Western Literate Culture Observers	
	Adults	Children
Happiness	92	92
Sadness	79	81
Anger	84	90
Disgust	81	85
Surprise	68	98
Fear		
from Anger/Disgust or Sadness	80	93
from Surprise	43	—
Number of Observers	189	130

towns; and, they had never worked for a Caucasian. Forty photographs were used of 24 different stimulus persons.

Table 14 shows the results for these visually isolated peoples, for both adults and children. The data have been organized in terms of the emotions expected on the basis of the Ekman, Friesen, and Tomkins FAST theory, which had been confirmed by the judgments of their literate culture subjects. The first row, for example, shows that when a face judged as *happy* in literate cultures was presented with two photographs usually judged in literate cultures as showing another emotion and a happy story was read to the observer, 92% of the observers chose the *happy* photograph. These data prove that the same facial behaviors are associated with the same emotions by these visually isolated members of a preliterate culture as by members of literate cultures. The only exception was in regard to fear which, as the table shows, was discriminated from sad, angry, disgusted, and happy faces, but not from surprised faces.

Ekman and Friesen (Ekman, 1972), also conducted a study on the posing of emotion, asking other visually isolated members of this New Guinea culture to show how their face would appear if they were the person described in one of the emotion stories that had been used in the judgment task.

Unedited videotapes of nine New Guineans were shown to 34 college students in the United States. Table 15 shows that except for the poses of fear and surprise (which the New Guineans had difficulty in discriminating), the students, who had never seen any New Guineans, accurately judged the emotion intended by their poses. This study further confirms the results from the recognition study reported in Table 14.

TABLE 15

Percent Correct Judgments by U.S.
Observers of New Guineans' Intended
Emotions

Happiness	73
Anger	51
Disgust/Contempt	46
Sadness	68
Surprise	27
Fear	18

These findings on both the recognition and posing of emotion by members of a preliterate culture strongly support the hypothesis that there is a pan-cultural element in the facial behavior associated with emotion. The only way to dismiss such evidence would be to claim that even these New Guineans who had not seen movies, who did not speak or understand English or Pidgin, who had never worked for a Caucasian, still had *some* contact with Westerners, sufficient contact for them to learn to recognize and simulate the culture-specific, uniquely Western facial behaviors employed with each emotion. Though it is true these subjects had some contact with Westerners, the argument seems implausible. The criteria for selecting these subjects should decrease the probability that they could have learned such a hypo-thesized "foreign" set of facial behaviors well enough not only to recognize them, but also to display a "foreign" set of behaviors as well as those to whom the behaviors were native. Further, Ekman and Friesen reported that the women in the New Guinean culture, who are considered to have even less contact with Westerners than the men, did just as well as the men in recog-nizing emotions.[38]

---

[38] In a study of another preliterate culture in New Guinea (the Dani), which is considerably more isolated than the Fore, essentially the same results were found (Ekman, 1972; Ekman, Heider, Friesen, & Heider, in preparation).

The best rebuttal of the culture-specific view underlying such skepticism comes from new evidence gathered with spontaneous, not posed, behavior and based on measures of the repertoire of facial behavior rather than on observers' judgments. The study, conducted by Ekman and his associates jointly with Lazarus and his associates, compared Japanese and American subjects. The purpose of the study was to determine whether the same facial behaviors occurred in the same emotion-eliciting circumstances in subjects within both cultures. Japan was selected for comparison with the United States because of the common belief that Japanese facial behavior is sufficiently different from that seen in the United States to mitigate against finding universals. Ekman and Friesen had hypothesized that when the subject was alone and not subject to the display rules governing facial appearance in public or social situations he would show the same basic repertoire of facial expression of emotion as his American counterpart. Another reason for selecting Japan was that it made feasible the use of an eliciting circumstance which would evoke essentially the same emotions in the two cultures. Averill, Opton, and Lazarus (1969) had previously conducted research in Japan to establish that the eliciting procedure of having subjects watch stress-inducing motion picture films led to self-reports of comparable emotion in Japan and the United States.

The design of this experiment and the results on the U.S. subjects were described in Chapter XVI, in connection with the measurement of components of facial behavior. We will briefly summarize the design and measurement procedure.

Twenty-five subjects in the U.S. and 25 subjects in Japan each individually watched a neutral and a stress-inducing film while seated alone in a room. Skin conductance and heart rate measures were taken with the subjects' knowledge, a videotape of their facial behavior without their knowledge.

Ekman, Friesen, and Tomkins' Facial Affect Scoring Technique (FAST) was employed to measure each movement of the face within each of three facial areas (brows/forehead, eyes/lids, lower face). This measurement procedure yields both frequency and duration scores for each of six emotions—happiness, anger, sadness, surprise, fear, and disgust—for each of the three areas of the face. Total face scores were also derived for any occurrences of facial activity in two or more areas at the same moment in time.

We have already reported (Chapter XVI) that the facial behavior shown by the Americans was very different in stress from that shown during the neutral film; the same finding was obtained for the Japanese. The crucial question to test the universality hypothesis, however, is whether the facial behavior shown in these two very different cultures was similar or not. For it would be quite

TABLE 16

*Ekman, Friesen, & Malmstrom's Frequency of Emotional Facial Behavior
Shown by American (N=25) and Japanese (N=25) Subjects
while Watching a Stress-Inducing Film*

	Total Face		Brows/Forehead		Eyes/Lids		Lower Face	
	U.S.	Japan	U.S.	Japan	U.S.	Japan	U.S.	Japan
Surprise	76	50	53	24	14	12	64	65
Disgust	61	48	16	13	17	12	31	38
Sadness	59	126	29	39	57	64	2	3
Anger	29	28	18	28	14	8	19	20
Happiness	8	14	0	0	8	8	8	22
Fear	2	1	0	0	7	0	0	0
Facial Behavior Which Was Not Emotion Specific	29	24	0	0	9	15	1	3
Rank Order Correlation	0.88 p <0.01		0.86 p 0.05		0.95 p 0.05		0.96 p 0.01	

possible for the facial behavior shown during stress and nonstress to differ
in both cultures, and yet for those differences to be dissimilar between cultures.

Table 16 shows that the repertoire of facial behavior shown during the
stress film was very similar for these two cultures. In the table, the frequency
measure of each type of emotional facial behavior across the 25 subjects in
each culture is listed; for example, when they totaled the whole face scores,
they found 76 surprise faces within the U.S. sample, 61 disgust faces, etc.
Rank order correlations were used for comparison of the two cultures, to see
whether the relative frequency of the different emotions was similar, and these
are quite high. The same calculations, made with the duration scores for each
emotion rather than the frequency scores shown in Table 16, yielded almost
identical results.

It must be acknowledge that Ekman, Friesen, and Malmstrom do not have
the definitive evidence to prove that they were actually measuring the facial
behavior associated with disgust, anger, fear, surprise, etc. In our discussion
of whether the Facial Affect Scoring Technique actually does measure
specific emotions, in Chapter XVI pages 117–118, we concluded that more

evidence was needed, although the results were encouraging. However, that determination is not crucial to the matter now under consideration. The Facial Affect Scoring Technique was successfully used to demonstrate the occurrence of different types of facial behavior in these two cultures. Even if the facial behavior were mislabeled by FAST (for example, if the behavior FAST labels *disgust* should be labeled *anger*, and vice versa), the evidence relevant to the universality question is whether the repertoire of these different types of facial behavior, whatever the label, is similar when subjects from these two cultures are in the same eliciting circumstance.

The extent of correspondence in the repertoire of facial behavior between these two cultures is remarkable. After all, these subjects live in cultures which are notoriously different in their public facial behavior. One of the elements which the investigators believe was crucial to obtaining this evidence of similarity, however, was that the subjects were not in a public situation. They did not know that their facial behavior was being observed, and thus no culture-specific display rules for managing their facial behavior should have been applicable.[39] After the subjects saw the stress film, a member of their own culture entered the room and conducted an interview about the experience. Although there are no results yet on this part of the experiment, Ekman, Friesen, and Malmstrom have inspected this public behavior and expect measurements of the facial behavior to show that in the interviews the Japanese subjects show very different facial behavior from the American subjects. During the interview, when display rules should apply, the Japanese appear to have engaged in masking, by showing happy faces when their Japanese interviewer asked them about their experience, while the Americans typically did not cover signs of negative affect when they talked with their American interviewer.

Many further interesting cross-cultural comparisons can be made from the data in this experiment; (e.g., is the relationship between the facial behavior and the physiological measures of arousal the same in the two cultures?); these are in progress. But it is the results shown in Table 16 which are most relevant to the fundamental question of whether there are any universals in the facial behavior associated with emotion. This experiment further confirms

---

[39] The success of this experiment may also be due to two other factors. (1) The measurement system did not describe just one type of facial behavior but was intended to measure facial behavior associated with six different emotions, so that even if the stress film elicited different emotions across the subjects, as long as these were different from the emotions elicited by the neutral film, accurate results could be obtained. (2) There was independent evidence (from the psychophysiological data and the self-reports) to indicate that the eliciting circumstance did call forth emotional reactions in the subjects.

the evidence for universals, which was found in the studies which utilized a judgments approach to show that observers associate the same emotion with the same facial behavior across cultures (Tables 13, 14, 15).

The evidence of a pan-cultural element does not imply the absence of any cultural differences in the face and emotion. It implies that we must look not at the particular facial behaviors associated with emotion but elsewhere for those differences. Ekman (1972), and Ekman and Friesen (1967b, 1969b) have suggested that cultural differences will be manifest in the circumstances which evoke an emotion, in the action consequences of an emotion, and in the display rules which govern the management of facial behavior in particular settings. Izard (1969, 1971) has hypothesized that cultural differences reside in attitudes about emotion, and has found different responses between Japanese and Western subjects to the questions, "What emotion do you least understand?", and "What emotion do you most dread?". He is also studying the responses to questions concerning the eliciting circumstances and the consequences of showing a particular facial behavior, but this work is not yet reported.

SUMMARY

The same emotions were judged for the same facial behaviors by observers from different cultures, in experiments which had many different stimuli of many different stimulus persons, and many different groups of observers, from 14 cultures or nations. Similar results were obtained with visually isolated, preliterate, New Guinea observers. A comparable repertoire of facial behavior was found in a study which measured the facial behavior shown by Japanese and American subjects while they watched a stress-inducing film. Together these findings provide *conclusive* evidence of a pan-cultural element in facial behavior and emotion. This element must be the particular association between movements of specific facial muscles and emotion concepts, since the results obtained require that in every culture some of the same facial behaviors be recognized and interpreted as the same emotion. There may well be such a pan-cultural element for more than the six emotions reported; and, in terms of the New Guinea group where visual isolation was obtained, the results were similar for only five emotions. It should be noted that these emotions for which there is pan-cultural evidence are not simply a random choice of possible emotion categories, but include most of the emotion categories most consistently emerging in one culture from the work of investigators who had focused on establishing the categories of emotion which can be judged from facial behavior (*see* Chapter XIII, Table 2).

Similarities in the association of facial behaviors with emotion concepts can be explained, from a number of nonexclusive viewpoints, as being due to evolution, innate neural "programs," or learning experiences common to human development (i.e., F. Allport, 1924; Asch, 1952; Huber, 1931; Izard, 1969, 1971; Izard & Tomkins, 1966; Peiper, 1963; Tomkins, 1962, 1963). The findings are consistent with studies of the facial behavior of blind compared to sighted children discussed earlier (Chapter XVI), and with recent illustrative films gathered in a number of cultures by Eibl-Eibesfeldt (1970). The choice among the different viewpoints as to the basis for facial muscles being related to emotion will require further research, particularly on early development and possibly also in studies utilizing brain stimulation in relation to facial activity.

The finding of cross-cultural similarities can help clarify the relationship discussed earlier of posed behavior to spontaneous behavior (*see* Chapters II, VII, XV). If, as Landis, and later Hunt, argued, posed behavior is a conventional language—socially learned and unrelated to real emotion—then it would be logical to expect, as they did, that poses would be judged differently across cultures. The fact that posed facial behavior was similarly judged across cultures, and that not only were Western poses understood by New Guineans, but New Guinea poses were understood by Westerners, requires either that these conventionalized facial behaviors were, inexplicably, learned the same way in all 14 cultures, or that Landis and Hunt were wrong, and that posed facial behavior resembles and grows out of spontaneous facial behavior. Our view is that posed facial behavior is similar to, if perhaps an exaggeration of, those spontaneous facial behaviors which are shown when the display rules to deintensify or mask emotion are not applied (*see* page 106). Posed behavior is thus an approximation of the facial behavior which spontaneously occurs when people are making little attempt to manage the facial appearance associated with intense emotion.

The findings of cross-cultural similarities in the face and emotion contradict the views of LaBarre and Birdwhistell, and support the claims of F. Allport, Asch, Darwin, Tomkins, and part of what Klineberg said. There seems little basis for disputing the evidence that for at least five emotion categories, there are facial behaviors specific to each emotion, and that these relationships are invariant across cultures. Two major empirical questions remain. What might account for these invariants in facial behavior; neurophysiology, constants in early learning for all humans, evolution, etc.? In what ways does facial behavior associated with emotion differ across cultures; by what means and to what extent do social-cultural determinants influence what evokes an emotion, the rules governing the visible display of emotion in the face, and the interpersonal consequences of such facial behavior?

PART FOUR

Final Considerations

CHAPTER XX

Research in Progress and Implications for Theory

As explained in the Introduction, there are many more areas of investigation about the human face and emotion than those we have examined. Two areas of study—children and nonhuman primates—were excluded both because there has been insufficient research and because some of the methodological problems are quite different from those encountered in the study of the human adult. However, three other lines of investigation currently being explored are raising highly pertinent questions; although it would be premature to discuss the results we can indicate the questions being asked.

The first area is concerned with the relationship between the facial behavior associated with emotion and other behavior shown in the face. Are there particular facial behaviors which are not specific to any one emotion, but which may provide information about matters other than emotion? The face can provide gestural information, such as a wink. The face can be used to illustrate speech during conversation; for example, the brows may be used to accent a word or phrase. Also, the face can engage in various instrumental acts, such as sniffing and lip biting. Do these facial behaviors relate to, overlap with, or employ different muscular movements than the facial behaviors associated with emotion?

A second area of study concerns the interactive consequences of facial behavior. Are there any regularities in the interactive behavior of those who perceive a particular facial behavior associated with emotion? Is there a special class of facial behaviors which function as regulators to manage the back and forth flow of interaction during conversation? At present the only regulators which have been extensively studied are eye-contacts. Are there more such discriminable, specifiable facial behaviors; and are they redundant, or perhaps additional consequences of facial behavior associated with emotion?

A third area is the study of individual differences in observers of emotion. Studies in progress suggest that differences among people in ability to recognize emotions in others are related to their own facial behavior, varying with whether they themselves furnish many or few distinctive facial behaviors. Another line of study in progress has revealed that individuals differ not so much in their ability to interpret all emotions, but in their ability to recognize specific emotions, and that deficiencies are related to long-standing personality characteristics and/or mood. Further, the ability to judge emotion may vary with the observers' circumstances, particularly if the faces judged are ambiguous or show blends.

We have deliberately refrained from discussing theories of emotion, except to indicate generally the basis for definition provided by each (Chapter I). We have chosen instead to analyze and integrate the evidence available about the relationship between the face and emotion. As we have seen, there is now considerable evidence that the face provides information about emotion. This evidence has implications for theories of emotion. We will briefly trace some of the developments in theories of emotion, and point out the implications of our findings.

Mandler (1962) has said that William James (1890) turned thinking about emotion upside down. Prior to James, the view was that what a man felt, thought, imagined, etc., led to certain emotions which were then registered in visceral reactions. James proposed just the reverse, that arousal of emotion produced a visceral reaction, and it was our awareness of that visceral reaction which was the experience of emotion. Cognition followed but did not lead or determine the visceral reaction. Lange proposed a similar view in 1885. This theory requires that the viscera can (a) provide the information necessary for distinguishing among emotions, (b) furnish this emotion-specific information to the person through an effective feedback loop so that he can know how he feels, and (c) change as rapidly as the changes in felt emotion. Cannon (1929) criticized the James-Lange theory of emotion, pointing out that visceral reactions do not provide sufficient information; the feedback from the viscera is diffuse, not precise; the viscera respond slowly; and there is little evidence to show that visceral reactions differ for each emotion.

Schacter (Schacter & Singer, 1962) re-established a steering role for cognition. He held that while visceral reactions are necessary for emotion they are not sufficient. Rather, it is cognition of the situation that provides the necessary information to distinguish one emotion from another, which can change rapidly, and by which we have feedback about how we feel. Schacter's theory, which is one of the dominant views of emotion in psychology today, thus fills with cognition the informational breach left by the visceral theory; but his theory takes no account of the informational properties of facial behavior.

The evidence we have discussed suggests that the face can provide differential information to those who measure it, to those who simply see it and probably, therefore, also to those who show it, through feedback from their own facial muscles. The face might also fill the informational gap left by a solely visceral theory of emotion, distinguishing one emotion from another, changing rapidly, and providing feedback about what is occurring to the person. We do not mean to suggest that cognition is irrelevant to emotion, nor necessarily that it takes a second place to facial behavior, but that we must reconsider theories of emotion to include not just visceral-physiological arousal and cognition, but the role of facial behavior as well. Three theories to date have made that attempt (Gellhorn, 1964; Plutchik, 1962; Tomkins, 1962, 1963).

CHAPTER XXI

Conclusion

The research findings presented in Part Three have shown that many of the fundamental questions which have been asked about the face and emotion during the last 55 years have been answered. Consistent evidence emerged when we applied the methodological framework developed in Part Two to evaluating, reanalyzing, and integrating findings from experiments conducted over the years. Many of the fundamental issues are settled, or nearly settled. Many more new, complex, and exciting questions can now be asked about the face and emotion.

Because of the disjunctive history of research on the face and emotion, many investigators have not profited from either the successes or failures of earlier work. Some of the questions answered earlier were asked again, as if for the first time. Our integration of past and recent findings in the context of seven key substantive questions should serve to eliminate such needless repetition. Also, investigators have at times persisted in utilizing research designs which earlier investigators had found to be defective. Our discussion of the conceptual ambiguities and methodological decisions which should be considered in planning further research may reduce this type of repetition. We now know enough about the face and emotion to cease asking questions which have already been answered, and to cease asking questions in ways which obscure any answer.

The information we now have about the face and emotion opens rather than closes this area of research, for the information now available represents but a beginning, an encouraging beginning, in understanding this complicated phenomenon. A multitude of intriguing questions must be answered if we are to comprehend fully the relationship between facial behavior and emotion. The time seems especially ripe for a resurgence of research on the human face. The legacy of pessimism initiated by the negative results of Landis and

Sherman, which survived despite repeated criticism of their shaky experiments and was amplified by reviewers of the literature who apparently misinterpreted some studies or were misinformed, should now be dissipated. The availability of inexpensive equipment for recording facial behavior (videotape), the appearance of three new methods for actually measuring facial behavior (Chapter XVI), and current interest in the face from those considered specialists in nonverbal communication, psychotherapy research, human ethology, early child development, social interaction, and education of the handicapped, should make research on the face and emotion a lively, active field in the coming decade.

In closing, we will briefly describe the answers which emerged from our separate consideration of each substantive question, attempting now to interweave some of the findings. We will also summarize some of the unsettled issues and raise some of the interesting new questions which await further research.

When people look at the faces of other people, they can obtain information about happiness, surprise, fear, anger, disgust/contempt, interest, and sadness (Chapter XIII). *They can also describe the information they obtain in terms of dimensions such as pleasant-to-unpleasant, active-to-passive, and intense-to-controlled* (Chapter XIV). *Impressions about whether someone is angry, happy, sad, etc., can be related to particular movements and positions of the face* (Chapter XVII).

Can those who see the face obtain information about more categories of emotion or about more dimensions of emotion than those listed? When people view the face, do they tend to think about the information they obtain more in terms of categories or of dimensions? What is the relationship between the categories and dimensions; are they redundant; can one be derived from the other, or do they refer to different facial behavior? Which provides more differentiated information? What cluster of words may be contained within a category, as, for example, the category *fear*; which are synonyms; which define its boundaries with another category, such as *surprise*; and which, although similar in general meaning, vary in intensity, such as "apprehensive," "afraid," "terrified"?

It is evident that the face can provide information about the presence of two emotion categories at the same instant in time or in rapid sequence. Are there specific words in our vocabulary which describe each of these blends, or do we need to refer to them as happy-angers, or sad-disgusts? Are there primary emotion words which describe single emotions apparent in the face, and secondary emotion words which describe the presence in the face of two or more of the primary emotions? Is it possible to specify the particular facial components of an affect blend? Can the anger-surprise blend, for example, be shown by an anger brow with a surprise mouth, and just as well with a surprise brow and an anger mouth?

No one area of the face was found to be superior in predicting how those who saw the face would describe all emotions. But, is one area of the face typically more informative for a particular emotion; for example, the lower face for disgust, the brows/forehead for surprise? Are there differences between persons in their use of one or another part of the face to convey a particular emotion or all emotions; if so, are such differences idiosyncratic, or related to ethnicity, social class, culture, or personality? Is there one part of the face which typically provides more information about all or some emotions in particular social settings, for example, when people are trying to conceal their feelings, is there one area of the face which is less subject to control? Do some people tend to regard or weigh one area of the face more than another in reaching their impressions about emotion?

The face can provide accurate information. Such information can be interpreted, without any special training, by those who see the face (Chapter XV). *It is also possible to measure facial behavior directly, and to obtain accurate information from the measurements* (Chapter XVI). *The particular facial behaviors which distinguish one emotion from another have been described and validated for some emotions. Accurate information can be obtained from the face alone without any knowledge of the context in which the facial behavior occurs, although in life the face is almost always seen within a context which also can provide accurate information. If the information from the face and context are of equal clarity but discrepant, it is possible for either the face or context to dominate the impression which is formed* (Chapter XVIII). *The best evidence that the face provides accurate information about spontaneous emotional behavior is limited to the gross distinction between positive and negative feelings; only with posed behavior do we have solid evidence of accurate information about specific emotions.*

Is it often possible for accurate information about specific emotions, such as anger, fear, disgust, sadness, to be derived from spontaneously occurring facial behavior, or can only the more simple distinction between positive and negative emotions be accurately obtained from most spontaneous facial behavior? Are there differences between individuals in terms of how often their facial behavior provides accurate information about emotion; and if so, are such differences associated with age, sex, ethnicity, social class, or personality? Are there certain types of social settings in which the face is more or less likely to provide accurate information? Is it possible to distinguish facial behavior in which the person is simulating an emotion in order to convey a false message to others from facial behavior in which the person does feel as he looks; or can we only tell from the face what the person wants us to think he feels?

How does the face compare with other behavioral channels, in terms of providing accurate information about emotion? Is the face usually redundant with the emotional information conveyed by voice, words, or retrospective self-report? Is the face usually redundant with psychophysiological measures of emotion; does the face provide more or less differentiated information than psychophysiological data? Do individuals differ in terms of which channel is most responsive or most reliable: facial behavior, body movements, voice, words, or psychophysiological responses?

When information provided by the face is discrepant with information provided by other behavioral modalities or the social setting, are there any regularities in how such discrepancies are mediated? Is the message gleaned from the emotion shown in the face, or from the characteristics of the setting or persons, or from all three? For example, if the face shows happiness, the setting is a hospital ward for severely ill persons, and the person showing the happiness is a middle-class, adult, white, male relative of the sick patient, will observers typically discount the happiness as a social mask and interpret the total information as sadness? And does this vary with emotion, person, and setting? Do observers differ in terms of preferential crediting of the face when information from the contextual source is discordant? If there are some people who characteristically credit facial information, what distinguishes them from those who do not; might this be more characteristic, for example, of the child than the adult?

While measurements of facial behavior have accurately discriminated the eliciting circumstances in which the behavior was shown, these measurements are relevant to only a few emotions. Can systematic measurement of facial behavior accurately distinguish a variety of emotion-eliciting circumstances for many different emotions, such as happiness, sadness, fear, anger, disgust, surprise, interest? How many different movements within each facial area are relevant for distinguishing each emotion; and how many different facial areas need to be measured to detect each emotion? Are there stable individual differences in terms of the particular facial area or movements within an area which will be most characteristic of a particular emotion, or across emotions? Does the measurement of facial behavior need to take account of the age of the persons; for example, are younger children able to show all of the facial wrinkling presumably relevant to measuring particular emotions? Do the procedures for measuring facial behavior offer any possibilities for training people to become more accurate judges of emotion?

There is one fundamental aspect of the relationship between facial behavior and emotion which is universal for man: the association between the movements of specific facial muscles and specific emotions. This has been found true for the facial appearance associated with anger, sadness, happiness, and disgust, and perhaps also for surprise and fear (Chapter XIX).

Are there more emotions which are associated pan-culturally with specific muscular movements? Are there emotions which are culture-specific, in that a distinguishable set of muscular movements is associated with the emotion by all members of one culture but not of another? Are there particular affect blends which occur with high frequency across cultures, as, for example, fear-surprise or happiness-interest; and are there particular affect blends which are culture-specific, rarely appearing in more than one or two cultures, such as happiness-sadness, disgust-interest?

Are there any universal elicitors, calling forth the same facial behavior across cultures, or are the elicitors of emotion learned or modified by learning in a culturally variable fashion? Are there any behavioral consequences which are universally found with particular facial behaviors; for example, is there a high probability of some type of flight movement consequent to a fear facial behavior, or are such behavioral consequences culture-specific?

We have hypothesized that there are culture-specific display rules, which dictate how facial behavior is to be managed in particular social settings, by intensifying, deintensifying, neutralizing, or masking facial behavior associated with emotion. What are these rules, how are they acquired—with what level of specificity in terms of the characteristics of the social situation and persons to which they apply? When a management technique is applied to the same facial behavior in two cultures (perhaps for different persons in different situations) is the resultant facial behavior similar? For example, if in culture X the display rule for adult males is to deintensify sadness at funerals, and in culture Y the display rules for adult female is to deintensify sadness when hearing about the husband's intended prolonged departure, is the facial appearance of the deintensified sadness the same in both cultures? We have hypothesized that deintensification may be accomplished in different ways: by fragmenting the facial behavior, so that movements are seen in only one facial area rather than across facial areas; by the time reductions, so that facial behavior is visible for a brief instant; or by a miniaturization, so that the excursion of the facial muscular movements is lessened. Are these techniques and the resulting facial appearance similar across cultures, even though the occasion for their use may differ? Can we recognize a deintensified or a masked emotion, regardless of culture, even without being able to specify why the management of the face occurred, or what the behavioral consequences might be?

Mandler, almost a decade ago, called for more research on the face and emotion. He said:

> It is rather surprising that facial expression has rarely been used in controlled studies of emotion, that is as a dependent variable in conjunction with some of the other emotional variables . . . if people can make such reliable judgments [Mandler was referring to the evidence that observers can accurately judge facial behavior], then psychologists also should be able to do so and to use expressive behavior more consistently in the laboratory. We might then have a reliable and useful dependent variable for the study of the whole emotional complex (1962, p. 307).

We now know more about the face, there is now more evidence to show that the face can and does provide information about emotion, and there are now some new alternative ways to measure the face. We would forecast that not only will study of the face be useful, but that full understanding of emotion depends upon understanding of the face.

Bibliography

Abelson, R. P. & Sermat, V. Multidimensional scaling of facial expressions. *Journal of Experimental Psychology*, 1962, **63**, 546–554.

Allport, F. H. *Social psychology*. Boston: Houghton Mifflin, 1924.

Arnold, M. B. *Emotion and personality*. New York: Columbia University Press, 1960.

Asch, S. E. *Social psychology*. Englewood Cliffs, N.J.: Prentice Hall, 1952.

Averill, J. R., Opton, E. M., Jr., & Lazarus, R. S. Cross-cultural studies of psychophysiological responses during stress and emotion. *International Journal of Psychology*, 1969, **4**, 88–102.

Bell, C. *The anatomy and philosophy of expression as connected with the fine arts* (4th ed.). London: John Murray, 1847.

Birdwhistell, R. L. The kinesic level in the investigation of the emotions. In P. H. Knapp, M.D. (Ed.), *Expression of the emotions in man*, Chapter 7, Part II. New York: International Universities Press, 1963.

Black, H. Race and sex factors influencing the correct and erroneous perception of emotion. *Proceedings of the 77th Annual Convention of the American Psychological Association*, 1969, 363–364.

Blurton-Jones, N. G. Criteria used in describing facial expressions. Unpublished manuscript, Department of Growth and Development, University of London, 1969.

Boring, E. G. & Titchener, E. B. A model for the demonstration of facial expression. *American Journal of Psychology*, 1923, **34**, No. 4, 471–485.

Boucher, J. D. Facial displays of fear, sadness and pain. *Perceptual and Motor Skills*, 1969, **28**, 239–242.

Boucher, J. D. & Ekman, P. A replication of Schlosberg's evaluation of Woodworth's scale of emotion. Paper read at the Western Psychological Association, Honolulu, 1965.

Bruner, J. S. & Tagiuri, R. The perception of people. In G. Lindzey (Ed.), *Handbook of social psychology*, Vol. 2. Reading, Mass.: Addison-Wesley, 1954. Pp. 634–654.

Buck, R., Savin, V. J., Miller, R. E., & Caul, W. F. Nonverbal communication of affect in humans. *Proceedings of the 77th Annual Convention of the American Psychological Association*, 1969, 367–368.

Campbell, D. T. & Fiske, D. W. Convergent and discriminant validation by the multitrait-multimethod matrix. *Psychological Bulletin*, 1959, **56**, 81–105.

Cannon, W. B. *Bodily changes in pain, hunger, fear and rage* (2nd ed.). New York: Appleton, 1929.

Coleman, J. C. Facial expressions of emotion. *Psychological Monograph*, 1949, **63** (1, Whole No. 296).

Darwin, C. *The expression of the emotions in man and animals*. London: John Murray, 1872.

Dashiell, J. F. A new method of measuring reactions to facial expression of emotion. *Psychology Bulletin*, 1927, **24**, 174–175.

Davis, R. C. The specificity of facial expressions. *Journal of General Psychology*, 1934, **10**, 42–58.

Dickey, E. C. & Knower, F. H. A note on some ethnological differences in recognition of simulated expressions of the emotions. *American Journal of Sociology*, 1941, **47**, 190–193.

Drag, R. M. & Shaw, M. E. Factors influencing the communication of emotional intent by facial expressions. *Psychometric Science*, 1967, **8**, 137–138.

Dunlap, K. The role of eye-muscles and mouth-muscles in the expression of the emotions. *Genetic Psychology Monograph*, 1927, **2**, 199–233.

Dusenbury, D. & Knower, F. H. Experimental studies on the symbolism of action and voice: I. A study of the specificity of meaning in facial expression. *Quarterly Journal of Speech*, 1938, **24**, 424–435.

Eibl-Eibesfeldt, I. *Ethology, the biology of behavior*. New York: Holt, Rinehart & Winston, 1970.

Ekman, P. Body position, facial expression, and verbal behavior during interviews. *Journal of Abnormal and Social Psychology*, 1964, **68**, 295–301.

Ekman, P. Communication through nonverbal behavior: A source of information about an interpersonal relationship. In S. S. Tomkins & C. Izard (Eds.), *Affect, cognition, and personality* (Chapter XIII). New York: Springer Press, 1965. Pp. 390–442. (a)

Ekman, P. Differential communication of affect by head and body cues. *Journal of Personality and Social Psychology*, 1965, **2** (5), 725–735. (b)

Ekman, P. Universals and cultural differences in facial expressions of emotion. *Nebraska Symposium on Motivation*, University of Nebraska Press, 1972.

Ekman, P. & Bressler, J. In P. Ekman, Progress report to National Institute of Mental Health, Bethesda, Md., 1964.

Ekman, P. & Friesen, W. V. Progress report to National Institute of Mental Health, Bethesda, Md., 1965.

Ekman, P. & Friesen, W. V. Head and body cues in the judgment of emotion: A reformulation. *Perceptual and Motor Skills*, 1967, **24**, 711–724. (a)

Ekman, P. & Friesen, W. V. Origin, usage and coding: The basis for five categories of nonverbal behavior. Paper presented at the Symposium on Communication Theory and Linguistic Models, Buenos Aires, 1967. (b)

Ekman, P. & Friesen, W. V. Nonverbal behavior in psychotherapy research. *Research in Psychotherapy*, Vol. 3. American Psychological Association, 1968.

Ekman, P. & Friesen, W. V. Nonverbal leakage and clues to deception. *Psychiatry*, Februar y 1969, **32** (1), 88–105. (a)

Ekman, P. & Friesen, W. V. The repertoire of nonverbal behavior—Categories, origins, usage and coding. *Semiotica*, 1969, **1**, 49–98. (b)

Ekman, P. & Friesen, W. V. Constants across cultures in the face and emotion. *Journal of Personality and Social Psychology*, 1971, **17** (2), 124–129.

Ekman, P. & Friesen, W. V. *Man's face*, in preparation.

Ekman, P., Friesen, W. V., & Malmstrom, E. J. Facial behavior and stress in two cultures. Unpublished manuscript, Langley Porter Neuropsychiatric Institute, San Francisco, 1970.

Ekman, P., Friesen, W. V., & Tomkins, S. S. Facial affect scoring technique (FAST): A first validity study. *Semiotica*, 1971, **3** (1), 37–58.

Ekman, P., Heider, E., Friesen, W. V., & Heider, K. Facial expression in a preliterate culture. Manuscript in preparation.

Ekman, P. & Rose, D. In P. Ekman, Progress report to National Institue of Mental Health, Bethesda, Md., 1965.

Ekman, P., Sorenson, E. R., & Friesen, W. V. Pan-cultural elements in facial displays of emotions. *Science*, April 4, 1969, **164** (3875), 86–88.

Engen, T., Levy, N., & Schlosberg, H. A new series of facial expressions. *American Psychologist*, 1957, **12**, 264–266.

Feleky, A. M. The expression of the emotions. *Psychological Review*, 1914, **21**, 33–41.

Fernberger, S. W. Six more Piderit faces. *American Journal of Psychology*, 1927, **39**, 162–166.

Fernberger, S. W. False suggestion and the Piderit model. *American Journal of Psychology*, 1928, **40**, 562–568.

Frijda, N. H. The understanding of facial expression of emotion. *Acta Psychologica*, 1953, **9**, 294–362.

Frijda, N. H. Facial expression and situational cues. *Journal of Abnormal Social Psychology*, 1958, **57**, 149–154.

Frijda, N. H. Recognition of emotion. In L. Berkowitz (Ed.), *Advances in experimental social psychology*, Vol. 4. New York: Academic Press, 1968. (a)

Frijda, N. H. Emotion and recognition of emotion. Presented at the Third Symposium on Feelings and Emotions, Loyola University, Chicago, October 10–12, 1968. (b)

Frijda, N. H. & Philipszoon, E. Dimensions of recognition of emotion. *Journal of Abnormal Social Psychology*, 1963, **66**, 45–51.

Frois-Wittmann, J. The judgment of facial expression. *Journal of Experimental Psychology*, 1930, **13**, 113–151.

Fulcher, J. S. "Voluntary" facial expression in blind and seeing children. *Archives of Psychology*, 1942, **38**, No. 272.

Gellhorn, E. Motion and emotion: The role of proprioception in the physiology and pathology of the emotions. *Psychological Review*, 1964, **71**, 457–472.

Gitter, A. G. & Black, H. Perception of emotion: Differences in race and sex of perceiver and expressor. Technical Report No. 17, Boston University, 1968.

Gladstones, W. H. A multi-dimensional study of facial expressions of emotions. *Australian Journal of Psychology*, 1962, **14**, 95–100.

Goffman, Erving. *The presentation of self in everyday life.* New York: Doubleday, 1959.

Goffman, E. *Behavior in public places.* Glencoe: Free Press, 1963.

Goldberg, H. D. The role of "cutting" in the perception of motion pictures. *Journal of Applied Psychology*, 1951, **35**, 70–71.

Goodenough, F. L. The expression of the emotions in infancy. *Child Development*, 1931 **2**, 96–101.

Goodenough, F. L. Expression of the emotions in a blind-deaf child. *Journal of Abnormal and Social Psychology*, 1932–3, **27**, 328–333.

Goodenough, F. L. & Tinker, M. A. The relative potency of facial expression and verbal description of stimulus in the judgment of emotion. *Journal of Comparative Psychology*, 1931, **12**, 365–370.

Grant, N. G. Human facial expression. *Man*, 1969, **4**, 525–536.

Guilford, J. P. An experiment in learning to read facial expression. *Journal of Abnormal Social Psychology*, 1929, **24**, 191–202.

Haggard, E. A. & Isaacs, K. S. Micro-momentary facial expressions as indicators of ego mechanisms in psychotherapy. In L. A. Gottschalk & A. H. Auerbach (Eds.), *Methods of research in psychotherapy*. New York: Appleton-Century-Crofts, 1966.

Hanawalt, N. G. The role of the upper and the lower parts of the face as the basis for judging facial expressions: II. In posed expressions and "candid camera" pictures. *Journal of General Psychology*, 1944, **31**, 23–36.

Hastorf, A. H., Osgood, E. E., & Ono, H. The semantics of facial expressions and the prediction of the meanings of stereoscopically fused facial expressions. *Scandinavian Journal of Psychology*, 1966, **7**, 179–188.

Hebb, D. O. Emotion in man and animal: An analysis of the intuitive processes of recognition. *Psychological Review*, 1946, **53**, 88–106.

Honkavaara, S. The psychology of expression. *The British Journal of Psychology, Monograph Supplements*, XXXII, R. H. Thouless (Ed.). New York: Cambridge University Press, 1961.

Howell, R. J. & Jorgenson, E. C. Accuracy of judging emotional behavior in a natural setting—A replication. *Journal of Social Psychology*, 1970, **81** (2), 269–270.

Huber, E. *Evolution of facial musculature and facial expression*. Baltimore: John Hopkins Press, 1931.

Hulin, W. S. & Katz, D. The Frois-Wittmann pictures of facial expressions. *Journal of Experimental Psychology*, 1935, **18**, 482–498.

Hunt, W. A. Recent developments in the field of emotion. *Psychological Bulletin*, 1941, **38**, No. 5, 249–276.

Izard, C. E. The emotions and emotion constructs in personality and culture research. In R. B. Cattell (Ed.), *Handbook of modern personality theory*. Chicago: Aldine, 1969.

Izard, C. E. *The Face of Emotion*. New York: Appleton-Century-Crofts, 1971.

Izard, C. E. & Tomkins, S. S. Affect and behavior: Anxiety as a negative affect. In C. D. Spielberger (Ed.), *Anxiety and behavior*. New York: Academic Press, 1966. Pp. 81–125.

James, W. *The principles of psychology*. New York: Holt, 1890.

Jarden, E. & Fernberger, S. W. The effect of suggestion on the judgment of facial expression of emotion. *American Journal of Psychology*, 1926, **37**, 565–570.

Jones, H. The study of patterns of emotional expression. In L. Regment (Ed.), *Feelings and emotion*. New York: McGraw-Hill, 1950.

Kanner, L. Judging emotions from facial expressions. *Psychology Monograph*, 1931, **41**, (3, Whole No. 186).

Kauranne, U. Qualitative factors of facial expression. *Scandinavian Journal of Psychology*, 1964, **5**, 136–142.

Kiritz, S. A. & Ekman, P. The deviant judge of affect in facial expression: Affect-specific errors. Unpublished manuscript, Langley Porter Neuropsychiatric Institute, San Francisco, 1971.

Klineberg, O. *Race differences*. New York: Harper, 1935.

Klineberg, O. Emotional expression in Chinese literature. *Journal of Abnormal and Social Psychology*, 1938, **33**, 517–520.

Klineberg, O. *Social psychology.* New York: Henry Holt, 1940.

Kozel, N. J. Perception of emotion: Race of expressor, sex of perceiver, and mode of presentation. *Proceedings of the 77th Annual Convention of the American Psychological Association,* 1969, 39–40.

Kozel, N. J. & Gitter, A. G. Perception of emotion: Differences in mode of presentation, sex of perceiver, and role of expressor. Technical Report No. 18, Boston University, 1968.

LaBarre, W. The cultural basis of emotions and gestures. *Journal of Personality,* 1947, **16,** 49–68.

LaBarre, W. Paralanguage, kinesics, and cultural anthropology. Report for the Inter-disciplinary Work—Conference on Paralanguage and Kinesics. Bloomington: Indiana University, Research Center in Anthropology, Folklore, and Linguistics, May 1962, 58 pages.

Landis, C. Studies of emotional reactions: II. General behavior and facial expression. *Journal of Comparative Psychology,* 1924, **4,** 447–509.

Landis, C. Studies of emotional reactions: V. Severe emotional upset. *Journal of Comparative Psychology,* 1926, **6,** 221–242.

Landis, C. The interpretation of facial expression in emotion. *Journal of General Psychology,* 1929, **2,** 59–72.

Landis, C. & Hunt, W. A. *The startle pattern.* New York: Farrar, 1939.

Lange, C. G., *Ueber gemuthsbewegungen.* Leipzig: Theodor Thomas, 1887. (Original Danish publication 1885; English translation in C. G. Lange & W. James, *The emotions.* Baltimore: Williams & Wilkins, 1922.)

Langfeld, H. S. The judgment of emotions from facial expressions. *Journal of Abnormal and Social Psychology,* 1918, **13,** 172–184.

Lanzetta, J. T. & Kleck, R. Encoding and decoding of facial affect in humans. *Journal of Personality and Social Psychology,* 1970, **16** (1), 12–19.

Leventhal, H. & Sharp, E. Facial expressions as indicators of distress. In S. S. Tomkins & C. E. Izard (Eds.), *Affect, cognition and personality, empirical studies.* New York: Springer, 1965. Pp. 296–318.

Levitt, E. A. The relationship between abilities to express emotional meaning vocally and facially. In J. R. Davitz (Ed.), *The communication of emotional meaning.* New York: McGraw-Hill, 1964. Pp. 87–100.

Levy, P. K. The ability to express and perceive vocal communication of feeling. In J. R. Davitz (Ed.), *The communication of emotional meaning.* New York: McGraw-Hill, 1964. Pp. 43–55.

Mandler, G. Emotion. In *New directions in psychology*: I. New York: Holt, Rinehart & Winston, 1962. Pp. 267–343.

Munn, N. L. The effect of knowledge of the situation upon judgment of emotion from facial expressions. *Journal of Abnormal and Social Psychology,* 1940, **35,** 324–338.

Murphy, G., Murphy, L. B., & Newcomb, T. M. *Experimental social psychology* (Rev. ed.) New York & London: Harper, 1937.

Nummenmaa, T. *The language of the face. Jyvaskyla studies in education, psychology, and social research.* Jyvaskyla, Finland: Jyvaskylan Yllopistoyhdistys, 1964.

Nummenmaa, T. & Kauranne, U. *Dimensions of facial expression.* Report No. 20, 1958, Department of Psychology, Institute of Pedagogics (now University of Jyvaskyla).

Osgood, C. E. Dimensionality of the semantic space for communication via facial expressions. *Scandinavian Journal of Psychology*, 1966, **7**, 1–30.

Peiper, A. *Cerebral function in infancy and childhood*. New York: Consultants Bureau, 1963.

Plutchik, R. *The emotions: Facts, theories, and a new model*. New York: Random House, 1962.

Royal, D. C. & Hays, W. L. Empirical dimensions of emotional behavior. *Proceedings of the 15th International Congress of Psychology, Brussels*, 1957, **419**. (Published 1959).

Rubenstein, L. Facial expressions: An objective method in the quantitative evaluation of emotional change. *Behavior Research Methods and Instruments*, 1969, **1**, 305–306.

Ruckmick, C. A. A preliminary study of the emotions. *Psychology Monograph*, 1921, **30** (Nos. 134–9), 30–5.

Rump, E. E. Facial expression and situational cues: Demonstration of a logical error in Frijda's report. *Acta Psychologica*, 1960, **17**, 31–38.

Schacter, S. & Singer, J. E. Cognitive, social and physiological determinants of emotional state. *Psychological Review*, 1962, **69**, 379–399.

Schlosberg, H. A scale for the judgment of facial expression. *Journal of Experimental Psychology*, 1941, **29**, 497–510.

Schlosberg, H. The description of facial expressions in terms of two dimensions. *Journal of Experimental Psychology*, 1952, **44**, 229–237.

Schlosberg, H. Three dimensions of emotion. *Psychological Review*, 1954, **61**, 81–88.

Schulze, R. *Experimental psychology and pedagogy: For teachers, normal colleges and universities* (Translated by R. Pintner). New York: Macmillan, 1912.

Sebeok, T. A., Hayes, A. S., & Bateson, M. C. *Approaches to Semiotics*. Hague, Netherlands: Mouton, 1964.

Shepard, F. N. The analysis of proximities: Multidimensional scaling with an unknown distance function. *Psychometrica*, 1963, **27**, 125–140.

Sherman, M. The differentiation of emotional responses in infants: I. Judgments of emotional responses from motion pictures views and from actual observation. *Journal of Comparative Psychology*, 1927, **7**, 265–284. (a)

Sherman, M. The differentiation of emotional responses in infants: II. The ability of observers to judge the emotional characteristics of the crying of infants and of the voice of an adult. *Journal of Comparative Psychology*, 1927, **7**, 335–351. (b)

Stratton, G. M. The control of another person by obscure signs. *Psychological Review*, 1921, **28**, 301–314.

Stringer, P. Cluster analysis of non-verbal judgments of facial expressions. *British Journal of Mathematical Statistics of Psychology*, 1967, **20**, 71–79.

Stringer, P. Personal communication to N. H. Frijda, 1968. (a)

Stringer, P. Sequential proximity as the basis for similarity judgments of facial expressions. Mimeo, University College, London, 1968. (b)

Tagiuri, R. Person perception. In G. Lindzey & E. Aronson (Eds.), *The handbook of social psychology* (2nd ed.) Vol. 3, **23**. Reading, Mass.: Addison-Wesley, 1968.

Thompson, D. F. & Meltzer, L. Communication of emotion intent by facial expression. *Journal of Abnormal and Social Psychology*, 1964, **68**, 129–135.

Thompson, J. Development of facial expression of emotion in blind and seeing children. *Archives of Psychology*, 1941, **37**, No. 264.

Tomkins, S. S. *Affect, imagery, consciousness*. Vol. 1, *The positive affects*. New York: Springer, 1962.

Tomkins, S. S. *Affect, imagery, consciousness.* Vol. 2, *The negative affects.* New York: Springer, 1963.

Tomkins, S. S. & McCarter, R. What and where are the primary affects? Some evidence for a theory. *Perceptual and Motor Skills*, 1964, **18**, 119–158.

Triandis, H. C. & Lambert, W. W. A restatement and test of Schlosberg's theory of emotion with two kinds of subjects from Greece. *Journal of Abnormal and Social Psychology*, 1958, **56**: 3, 321–328.

Trujillo, N. P. & Warthin, T. A. The frowning sign multiple forehead furrows in peptic ulcer. *Journal of the American Medical Association*. August 5, 1968, **205**, No. 6, 218.

Vinacke, W. E. The judgment of facial expressions by three national-racial groups in Hawaii: I. Caucasian faces. *Journal of Personality*, 1949, **17**, 407–429.

Vinacke, W. E. & Fong, R. W. The judgment of facial expressions by three national-racial groups in Hawaii: II. Oriental faces. *Journal of Social Psychology*, 1955, **41**, 184–195.

Vine, I. Communication by facial-visual signals: A review and analysis of their role in face-to-face encounters. In J. H. Crook (Ed.), *Social behavior in animals and man.* London & New York: Academic Press, 1969.

Woodworth, R. S. *Experimental psychology.* New York: Henry Holt, 1938.

Zlatchin, C. & Ekman, P. Misperception of facial affect. Unpublished manuscript, Langley Porter Neuropsychiatric Institute, San Francisco, 1971.

Author Index

189